The Remarkable Life of
Henry Thomas Hamblin

Mystic and Successful Businessman

Mereo Books

2nd Floor, 6-8 Dyer Street, Cirencester, Gloucestershire, GL7 2PF
An imprint of Memoirs Books. www.mereobooks.com
and www.memoirsbooks.co.uk

The Remarkable Life of Henry Thomas Hamblin

ISBN: 978-1-86151-877-4

First published in Great Britain in 2023
by Mereo Books, an imprint of Memoirs Books.

Copyright ©2023

John Delafield has asserted his right under the Copyright Designs and Patents Act 1988 to be identified as the author of this work.

Cover Picture by the Author

A CIP catalogue record for this book is available from the British Library.
This book is sold subject to the condition that it shall not by way of trade or otherwise be lent, resold, hired out or otherwise circulated without the publisher's prior consent in any form of binding or cover, other than that in which it is published and without a similar condition, including this condition being imposed on the subsequent purchaser.

The address for Memoirs Books can be
found at www.mereobooks.com

Mereo Books Ltd. Reg. No. 12157152

Typeset in 11/15pt Century Schoolbook
by Wiltshire Associates.
Printed and bound in Great Britain

The Remarkable Life of
Henry Thomas Hamblin
Mystic and Successful Businessman

JOHN DELAFIELD

Based on his Autobiography "The Story of My Life"
and compiled by John Delafield, grandson of
Henry Thomas Hamblin

Henry Thomas Hamblin, 1873-1958, was a spiritual teacher from Sussex whose forward-thinking message was the importance of getting beyond thought to access our inner peace.

Other Books by John Delafield

Gliding Competitively (A&C Black)
A Life of Flying (Mereo Books)

CONTENTS

Introduction
Preface

PART 1

Chapter 1	Early Days	1
Chapter 2	School	8
Chapter 3	Technical School	15
Chapter 4	A Disturbing Experience	20
Chapter 5	Difficult Years	30
Chapter 6	I Leave Home	40
Chapter 7	More Wild Oats	49

PART 2

Chapter 8	I Return Home	63
Chapter 9	Important Moves	72
Chapter 10	Through the Dark Valley	82
Chapter 11	Again I Launch Out	91
Chapter 12	An Adventure in the West End	101
Chapter 13	Thus Far Shalt Thou Go	111
Chapter 14	I Retire from the Scene	119

PART 3

Chapter 15	I Give Up My Liberty	133
Chapter 16	Reaping	145
Chapter 17	The Start of the Science of Thought	154
Chapter 18	The Science of Thought – Huge Challenges	166
Chapter 19	The Science of Thought Review	177
Chapter 20	War Again	187
Chapter 21	After the War	198
	Afterword	210
	Epilogue	212

Introduction

The life experience of my grandfather, Henry Thomas Hamblin, often known as HTH, and the philosophy he developed, was principally of the omnipresence of God with a clear focus on the teachings of Jesus Christ. Although he had a broad appreciation of the power of other beliefs to help a searcher find God, he wrote that God was latent within every human being. In today's language he might have said that every human is 'hard-wired' to need God but that this feature must be activated. He would certainly say that God is with us now and always. He believed that health, happiness and a sense of achievement are the normal state for mankind, but that to achieve this state the individual needed to align with Cosmic Law, which he also referred to as The Truth.

Over his 45 years as a prolific author, the emphasis of Hamblin's work developed from suggesting to his readers how to change their lives through 'right thought' and faith to teaching them how to find a living consciousness of God within themselves. It was this process which led him to publishing a monthly magazine called *The Science of Thought Review* which endured for some 85 years before being re-orientated as a larger-sized printed magazine entitled *New Vision* (later to be called *Hamblin Vision)* which endured for a further 20 years and is now online only.

Hamblin's work continues to this day through the Hamblin Trust, which propagates the work he began in 1921, when he was in his mid-40s, and, in keeping with the times of 100 years later and now, in the new online environment, publishes *Hamblin Vision*, the magazine which follows the path established by the original *The Science of Thought Review*. Books are still available too. This new book has been compiled by his grandson, John Delafield, based on HTH's own works and is written just over 100 years after HTH launched into his life's work as a disciple of God. His work and advice became widely read and was followed by many.

His understanding of God, and the way one should live in harmony and peace, is timeless and this book seeks to encapsulate the life he lived and his understanding of God in a way that will appeal to and assist the reader be they of a religious persuasion or of none.

It was not all plain sailing for HTH, as this book sets out, and the first half of his life saw failure, ill health, family bereavement, as well as striking success. This experience was a crucial part of his development into a teacher, philosopher, mystic, and guide who was then able to help many others.

This book is based on HTH's own autobiography, *The Story of My Life*, (1947) and includes short sections of his other works, some of which he published earlier in his life as advice to his readers on how to follow the will of God and discover the Truth. The original text has been updated and clarified but the message of my grandfather, "HTH", endures.

The original *The Story of My Life* was published 11 years before he died. He dedicated the original book to his wife, Eva Elizabeth, with these words:

This book is dedicated to my dear wife who for forty-four years has been my great support and stay. Without her steadying influence, nothing which, under grace, has been achieved, would have been possible.

They were to have a further 11 years together before HTH died.

And he follows this dedication in the original book, *The Story of My Life*, with a note headed *Thanks* of which this is an abridged version:

My most grateful thanks are due to Sir Robert Bristow for so kindly writing his Introduction to this book. He has been a friend and supporter of the Science of Thought work for 12 years and is, therefore, in a position to comment as one ministered to. I can only see my work from the inside whereas he can view it as a whole and objectively.

Sir Robert Bristow (13 December 1880 – 3 September 1966) was a well-known British harbour engineer working in India, where he contributed to the development of the port of Kochi (Cochin). Bristow recounted his experiences in his book Cochin Saga, which is a valuable source of historiography of Kerala, the region in which Kochi is situated. He was also noted for his initiatives in founding the Lotus Club, the first inter-racial club in Kochi. He first encountered my work towards the end of his working life.

This following text is based on the Introduction by Sir Robert Bristow to the original The Story of My Life (1947) and has been revised by the Author.

Henry Thomas Hamblin (HTH) was born in 1873 at Walworth, Southeast London, of Kentish parents and was the second of two sons. His father was very religious, and his grandfather was a minister of the Baptist Church. His mother, although of diminutive size was reportedly "great of soul", ruled the family with benevolent autocracy. They were poor, very poor, like all those living around them in that era, and despite hard work, the only education that could be afforded for HTH was an elementary one, followed by a course in technology which proved to be of inestimable value to a youth then in his early years who was considered by his parents to be wayward.

His mother often reproached him by saying: "Unstable as water; thou shall not excel". Hardly confidence-giving. "Slacker," said his elder brother, but wiser heads might have recognised something better in the young boy who, at the age of nine, could attempt the writing of a newspaper and had already established himself as having the skills of an elocutionist.

The succeeding years gave little indication of an error in the family verdict. Henry "the wayward" moved from one poorly paid post to another, idled, had bouts of sickness and, before he was eighteen, had displayed more than the usual adolescent failings. At one point he might have qualified as a prodigal son, but always the pangs of regret followed his periods of indulgence, such that "Henry the sinner" became "Henry the saint" – until the next time.

He was inspired by books, and many of them fired his ambition, whilst books about the lives of the patriarchs prompted his spiritual imagination.

Overall, he must have been a young lad with huge aspiration, flushed with a youthful zest for life, and inspired by a worthy ambition to rise above the rut of his circumstances and, at heart, he was incurably religious.

A person's early environment, education and adolescent behaviour can often predetermine the course of their life, and in his autobiography, *The Story of My Life*, he possibly makes too much of his early transgressions. Youthful indulgences of one sort or another are inevitable. By contrast, selfishness, hypocrisy rather than indulgence, received the greater condemnation of Jesus and this would have been very much in Hamblin's consciousness.

From reading his book, one may feel that more details of his technical training would have been helpful in explaining the play of forces within him, but he says enough to reveal the inestimable value of a curious mind coupled with scientific accuracy as it related to his later endeavours.

Despite his lack of education, he was bolstered by boundless faith and courage, coupled with a shrewd business sense, and succeeded beyond all expectation.

He was not a genius, and millions of people have made good in the world with less promising assets. But Hamblin was surely unique in that, concurrently with a strenuous business life in his late 30s and early 40s, he demonstrated clearly that Christianity as a working faith is not only a code for decent men and women with a focus on the Hereafter, as Hamblin would have called it, but that God is around us and within us and is the fundamental reality. The teaching of Jesus represents a Divine Order for the world.

Human organisations come and go and today's scientific advances are the commonplace features of tomorrow: churches quarrel, dogmas die, but the Kingdom of God is changeless. God's laws are eternal, and He is the quintessence of Love, Wisdom, and Harmony.

In a myriad of ways, Hamblin exemplified and supplemented these principles in his writing and made it clear that that God himself does not punish but that the individual person punishes themselves by rejecting the teachings of Jesus who was the manifestation of God. He makes it clear that God does not demand servility but is pure Love and all he asks for is faith in that Love.

Hamblin said that if you seek Him in prayer the corollary is that you must have faith in Him. This faith is fundamental to the relationship. You must be sure that God knows your need even before you have tried to express it yourself. He makes it clear that no prayer goes unanswered, although the answer may be not what was anticipated; all prayer offered in faith will be answered in some form, he stresses.

Hamblin reminds the reader that Jesus travelled down the same road as us and poses that question: "We may believe in his teachings but are we truly in harmony with them?"

This is the juncture at which Hamblin identifies what he calls the "great mystery". He makes it clear that it is not by learning, devout thinking, feverish works or stoic courage that a person can find God in the sense of "knowing" God. And yet humans long to "know" in the spiritual sense, and this can underpin searches in the psychic arena and in other ways. Hamblin takes the view "Blessed are they who believe and yet have not seen", because the knowledge of God is born within us and should grow steadily throughout life, if cultivated. Thus, Jesus became the eternal example by demonstrating that only by the loss of self can God be found. Sacrifice all – gain all.

Hamblin was very clear on this and wrote:

To develop the inner self is to enter into a life of unlimited power;

the power to control oneself, one's life and one's circumstances. It is to enter into a wider, fuller, deeper, and richer life of overcoming, of achievement, of peace of mind, of surpassing joy and happiness.

- HT Hamblin, "Look Within"

At whatever age a person surrenders his or her "self" to God it is then that a re-birth takes place and one's real life in God begins.

One can question this view and say: "what is all this but the core teachings of many brands of Christianity?" At this juncture, Hamblin says very clearly that modern Christianity is a heterogenous compound of the teaching of Jesus interwoven with historic pagan-based doubts and fears, litanies, and supplications, credal theories, episcopal sanctions, papal bulls, worldly compromises and prejudices, all closely guarded by a priestly hierarchy. Strong views, but Hamblin does not condemn and says the churches are necessary and helpful for those who are succoured by them. He makes it clear that they proclaim the fundamental Truth as espoused by Jesus.

He says that his teaching is for all and that it knows no sect and no division and is one with the aspiration of all good people and of all nations of all time. Hamblin, in his various other works, sees the Light (the enlightenment) in Buddha, in Confucius, in Lao Tzu, in St. Theresa and others, but says that they are no substitute for the teachings of Jesus with its stress on the use of an individual's talents. Still less does he accept the cloistered seclusion of sanctuaries, the ivory towers of the highly religious, or the barbaric deeds of fanatics. He makes it clear that people are made in the image of God and that it is Jesus who has shown the way.

Hamblin states: "There can be no finite creed of an infinite faith". When creeds appear, true faith can be constrained; such is the burden of Hamblin's thought, but it reveals the foundations of his belief.

First, he says, comes purity of intention and self-dedication, reminding the reader that one cannot serve God and Mammon.

Either you trust God completely or you hedge your bets by having worldly alliances and a healthy bank balance but you restrict, thereby, your spiritual development. But, he says, your dedication must be active and bear fruit and, as with planting a fruit tree, much preparatory work has first to be done, requiring great patience, perseverance, faith, and courage. But the process of so doing will teach you forbearance and good will.

Other life experiences will follow naturally and lead to compassion developing which in turn will enable the person to subconsciously radiate the Love of God.

Hamblin states unequivocally that the key to this process is the Lord's Prayer, which is complete without qualification and the practice of it will reveal its majestic simplicity.

There is one other important factor in Hamblin's life, and that is a family bereavement that was so profound and sudden that it reached down to the very roots of his being. His youngest son died of an illness aged only 10 whilst away at boarding school. This would have been a trauma beyond imagination for most people but, looking at the tragedy now, it appears to have been part of the experience that helped to illuminate God to him. As the late Dean Inge wrote in his book *Personal Religion*, "Bereavement is the deepest initiation into the mysteries of human life... the sharpest challenge to our trust in God; if faith can overcome this, there is no mountain it cannot remove". Hamblin says that glimmerings of the Passion of Christ Jesus emerge, but we shrink from the irreverence of probing the ways of God. Does one need, he suggests, to surrender something dear at heart, one's worldly reputation or self-esteem, or one's pride of life and love of power, riches, and things we hold most dear, and the defensive armour we surround ourselves with and trust so earnestly? Do we?

Yes, says Hamblin, whatever is needed to complete one's faith in God will invariably involve a renunciation of something deeply personal to you. But whatever is surrendered to God will be magnified in some form and returned to you. He understood that Christianity is not only about ethics but of the transcendent power of God and the sharing of his life as demonstrated by Jesus. A powerful statement.

Where should we place Henry Thomas Hamblin in the long line of Christian seekers and finders? Perhaps it verges on the impertinent even to pose the question, but it is surely relevant. Consider all the facts; he was a poor man, uneducated by university standards, born into a life of obscurity, but by superhuman efforts of imagination he rose to wealth and an esteemed position in life whilst, all the time, he was aware of another "self" within him. And then in middle life he surrendered his material successes to follow his wider calling as a disciple of God. He was not to subscribe to any creed or religion but became a literal follower of God and an advocate of the simple teachings of Jesus Christ.

Hamblin was no haloed saint in the traditional sense of the term. He would say, "What I have done, or rather what has been done through me, can be done by any person on earth according to their gifts and personal faith".

His *The Story of My Life* (on which this new book is based) is a witness to this; he has gone out of his way to express his faults of character, his defects in education, his very human interest in all things, great and small. And when he describes his childhood, he does so as a child and not as an adult and at each stage of his life he expresses himself as the person he was at the time. He knows that he has been "moved by the Spirit to write this life-story". He shows us from the example of his own life the universality of Jesus, the unique Son of God.

Throughout his long life, Henry Thomas Hamblin, was supported through thick and thin by his wife, Eva Elizabeth Hamblin, but he makes scant mention of her in *The Story of My Life*, and it falls to me as their grandson to make amends in this rewritten version.

There is absolutely no doubt whatsoever that she was the "power behind the throne" and without her my grandfather's many enterprises, both in his early years and later as a writer, would have been impossible. She was a very wise person and always struck me as someone who provided huge stability and common sense and enabled Henry Thomas Hamblin to excel in his many chosen domains.

This picture was taken by me in about 1953 and shows them both at the entrance to the house they had built, which was then called Bosham House.

Preface

Henry Thomas Hamblin's preface to "The Story of My Life"

(Author's note: To ensure that the reader best understands Hamblin's views, this preface is little changed from the words he wrote in 1947.)

My belief is that life is good and that the Love of God is close to every individual throughout life.

I believe that there is a Divine pattern to each life and that this pattern is perfect. I believe also that the cause of many health issues during life can be caused by a failure to follow the Divine pattern and that, if we could but follow it, life would be greatly enhanced.

To my mind, humanity has drifted away from this Divine pattern which leads to disorder. The reality, by contrast, is that the Divine order is perfect. It has always been with us and permeates the Universe. It just awaits our recognition.

Jesus, when he preached, said (depending on the translation) *"Change your life because God's kingdom is near."* (Matthew 4.17). What this implies is "cease thinking thoughts which are at odds with the Divine pattern of your life and think, instead, of thoughts which align with the Divine pattern".

A person's life would be perfect as it is imagined in the mind of God. Sufferings, disorders, and difficulties of life are not solely the result of a departure from the Divine order but can be viewed as an attempt by God, as Infinite love, to bring us back into harmony with the Divine pattern.

Thus, we could view the sufferings and disharmonies which come to us on our departure from the Divine order not as punishments but simply Divine love in action trying to bring us back into a state of harmony. This harmony offers unspeakable joy.

Life should be love all the way and as Psalm 23.6 says: *"Surely goodness and mercy shall follow me All the days of my life; And I will dwell in the house of the LORD Forever"*.

When I was young, I was not taught this. If I had known then what I know now, my life might have been very different. If only, when I was eighteen years old or so, I could have had a book like those I published some 30 years later, it would have been a true Godsend. Alas, I had to find everything out for myself through experience and from some suffering.

My own mind is now clear on this, and I well know that thoughts arising from the sub-conscious can be primitive and need to be adapted and ideally exchanged completely for God-like thoughts, as so eloquently advocated by Jesus. If unredeemed thoughts are allowed to retreat to the subconscious unchanged then they can propagate and surface again. By contrast, if thoughts are changed for God-like ones then they in turn will propagate the work of God and the Holy Spirit.

Therefore, my advice, to paraphrase Jesus, is: *"Change your thoughts and align them with the Kingdom of Heaven and follow the Divine pattern in your life."*

Alas, when I was young, I knew nothing about the power of thought and did not appreciate that much depends on what we think and that feeling and emotion by themselves can have such a powerful influence. I did not know that having thoughts of resentment or hatred can destroy health, mental balance and even life itself. I did not know that just having negative thoughts can be enough to trigger negative action and medical disorders. I did not know that entertaining thoughts of fear can bring about the very things we fear. I did not know that negative thought can be destructive in the extreme.

I had no idea that proper thought control can enhance one's spiritual outlook and help bring one closer to God. I did not know that it is possible to change a negative thought into a Heavenly one.

I did not know how to cultivate a Christlike thought from a devilish one.

I did not know the harmful effect of negative thoughts and I did not know that Christlike thoughts can permeate one's whole being and bring one closer to God.

I did not appreciate the message of Jesus in advocating: "Change your minds and thoughts". If I had, I might have tried to do so, as I was sure that He was the one whose teaching we should follow. I could not understand the theologians who made things so difficult and complicated; I wondered how people could ever understand enough from this sort of teaching to move their lives closer to God.

I knew nothing about these things.

The result was that I found myself wallowing in a swamp of wrong thoughts for which I suffered to my detriment.

Now to the "if only" view. If only I had known of the power of right thinking, my early life could have been quite different. I could have been a far better son, brother, husband, and parent than I proved to be. Also, I could have been in a better position to help others.

This is not a complaint about life; I now realise that everything comes to pass at the right time, and I needed to learn the hard way to enable me to understand the issues and develop my own ideas about how best I could help others. There is a difference between learning from experience and learning from books. My life took me along the rough road full of potholes, but it was only after my work was well established that I came across the earlier writings of saints and mystics. Sometimes I wondered whether this could have been that the truth about God and life was withheld from the masses on the basis that "knowledge is power"? But perhaps that is a cynical view and it is certainly not a Christ-like one.

Therefore, what I have been guided to teach through my own writings is not new, but I have been enabled to present it in a simple and fresh way so that it can be readily understood by many. I have found it possible to speak and write about what I have been led to discover and to do so using the simplest of language and without dogma or creed.

I envisage a world moving ever closer to the true design of God, as taught by Jesus.

My life is a powerful yet simple story that will emerge as you read further into it.

I hope you find it inspirational.

PART 1

Chapter 1

Early Days

My father, Joseph Hamblin, was one of the sons of a Baptist minister. His father, my grandfather, could be described as a rather humble version of the preacher John Wesley, a British cleric (1703 to 1791) who was a well-known theologian and evangelist and the leader of Methodism, a revival movement within the Church of England at the time. My grandfather would hold services in the open air on village greens and often in the face of hostility. Like Wesley before him, he had narrow escapes from being stoned by a hostile audience but invariably a local blacksmith or other physically strong person would assume the role of his protector.

My mother was the daughter of the local coach and carriage builder.

My father did not follow in my grandfather's footsteps and neither did any of his brothers. He never once preached a sermon and was happiest being a member of the congregation. On the other hand, he was a man of prayer and in this capacity was content to lead a congregation in prayer if he had to. It was in private that he did the bulk of his praying. For example, on Sunday evenings he would conduct family worship in which we sang hymns, with him then reading a chapter from the Bible, after which he would pray earnestly for each member of the family by name.

And that was not the end of it. Late every evening, not just Sundays, my father would retire to his bedroom to pray for us children. We could hear his booming voice throughout the house as he implored God to save us from everlasting torment. These loud supplications could last an hour after which he would come downstairs for supper. Never once did he tell us exactly what he had been praying about.

This puzzled me and, when I was older, I used to wonder why, if God was a God of love as we had been taught, father should have to pray such a lot to prevent us ending up in the eternal fire of Hell? It made me curious.

Sunday, in those days, was akin to a religious Field Day. We children had to dress up tidily and be in Sunday School by 10am as a prelude to attending the service for "grown-ups" which would commence at 11am and could last until nearly 1pm. The torture of long sermons, not a word of which was comprehensible to me, was almost beyond endurance. What a relief it was to reach the end of the service when we could rush outside into the open air. After this it would be back to our home to a cold meal as, in those days, there was no cooking permitted on Sundays. But that was not the end of the day as we had then to hurry back to afternoon Sunday School for yet more talks about God.

I remember one man who made us endure his long talk. He took a sheet of paper without a mark on it and said that it represented our soul. Then he said that if our soul was like a clean sheet of paper, we would go to Heaven when we died. But if there was just one speck on it (and he made a small mark with a pencil) then, when we died, we would go straight to Hell and be tortured forever. I rather enjoyed it in a perverse sort of way!

After this second Sunday School of the day, we were permitted to go home for tea and after that the elder children and one parent would go to the evening Service in the church. The remaining parent would stay at home to protect the house from burglars, and also look after me, but no burglars ever came and if they had they could have left empty handed as we had nothing of value.

It was at around this time that I had my first experience of a poltergeist. This is the story: one Sunday evening, when my father and I were alone in the house, all the bells in the house began to ring violently. (This was in the days when each room had a bellpull which, by a series of cables, would activate a bell elsewhere in the house.) Naturally, we were both scared and bewildered and immediately assumed that someone had got into the house and was having fun with the bellpulls in each room. We searched the house from top to bottom but could not find anyone. I was frightened so I left it to my father to peer into cupboards and wardrobes, but he saw nothing which could have caused the issue.

Despite this searching, the bells kept on ringing with some energy, and I remember seeing the wires moving as though they were being tugged by a very strong man. To this day, I can still see in my mind the bells swinging more than I'd ever seen them do before. When a bell for a specific room rung, we would rush to the relevant room only to find it deserted. Then, as if playing a game, other bells from other rooms would then ring and, again, we would find no one there. Despite our zealous searching we found no cause for this. It never happened again for which my father and I were greatly relieved. We never did understand the event.

My father would probably have attributed the phenomena to the Devil, but nothing was ever said about it and the subject was made strictly taboo.

But I did not forget it; it would not be until some 50 years later that I had the chance to read further about such phenomena.

Whilst my mother spent her life at home, my father went off to London to seek his fortune in a city he believed to be paved with gold. He must have given up on the idea because next I remember him being in a humdrum job locally which was notable only for its meagre pay.

My mother was a remarkable woman and we called her "little mother" as she was only 4ft 10 inches tall, the same height as Queen Victoria. There was no doubt that she was the master of the house. Despite her stature, she ruled with a firm hand. If Father tried to assert himself, he would soon be frowned into submission.

It was similar with us children as we were ruled with a firm hand, although it would be more accurate to say with a well-used cane. But Father never caned us and would instead make excuses on behalf of us all.

Mother was skilled with the cane and my brother, 5 years older than me, was stoic under punishment, but by contrast when I was beaten, I screamed and naturally gained a reputation for being "the big noise" of the family. My sister was 4 years older than me, and I do not recall whether she was ever punished in the way we boys were.

Although mother wielded the cane, I think we probably loved her more than father; she had spirit and energy together with a sense of both fun and humour and she was the positive partner whereas Father played the negative part. It is always the positive people who attract.

Mother was very lovable despite her strict discipline, and it was quite clear that she adored children. She was generous to an extreme and was always helping someone. Despite the meagre family income, she always had money for God's work and every month she would take the whole of Father's slender earnings and put a tenth into a little linen bag which she would set aside for the church. The rest she divided up; portions for food, for clothes, for schooling and so on with each in its special bag. It was practical, simple, and it worked. She had no need of an accountant!

I do not know when my parents got married but I do know that their first home was in Walworth, south-east London. Shortly after they were married my father was baptised into the Baptist church. All of us children were born in the house with my own arrival being on 19th March 1873.

When I was aged two, we moved into a newly built house further away from the centre of London at Brockley. I was told that when we moved there it was in open country surrounded by fields growing market produce. I can remember walking in the countryside and my father once finding a ripe strawberry, which I consumed with great relish.

Now the area is a desolation of bricks, mortar, slates, and chimney pots.

It was when I was about four or five that I first remember encountering negative thinking. It was like this; I noticed that when we had visitors, and they were asked how they were, they never said that they were well and what most of them said was that they were not very well, neither ill nor well. A favourite expression I recall was: "I'm not *very* well, no, I am only in the middlings". As they said this, they adopted a melancholy expression and tried to look as resigned as possible to their condition which duly ensured they received a chorus of sympathy.

I was an observant child and must have made a mental note of this and I thought it was time I too received some sympathy. Consequently, when in due course we had a lady visitor, and I was introduced to her, she asked: "Well little man, how are you today?" I thought I would copy the "grownups" and in response screwed up my face, imitating what I had observed others do, and looked as sad as possible and replied: "Oh, I am only in the middlings today, thank you".

To my surprise, instead of evoking a chorus of sympathy, they all burst out laughing. "Oh, how funny", they said. "Henry says he's only in the middlings. Ha! Ha! Ha!" I was puzzled and had no idea why they laughed at me as I was only copying what they said. I gave up puzzling about it and let the matter rest. In later years I began to understand the mind-set behind these negative remarks.

I was young, of course, and there were many things I did not comprehend. I never made a point of trying to be funny and yet many of the things I did provoked laughter from my audience, which mystified me.

The story of the butter dish comes to mind. Our pocket money was one penny a week (pre-decimal money with one penny being 1/240th of a £) and my sister and I decided to buy a birthday present for our mother and drew out our precious savings that amounted to one shilling (pre-decimal money – 5p in decimal coinage.) It was a huge amount of money to us then, and we thought carefully about how best to spend it in buying a gift for our mother. We shopped in Broadway Pavement, as it was called, and we were after a bargain. We tried many shops and disappointed many shopkeepers until we spotted a glass butter dish. The price was cut although the glass was not cut-glass! The shopkeeper wanted one shilling, which was all we had, and so we offered the man nine pence. My sister and I thought it was a very fair offer, but the shopkeeper did not. We finally agreed a price of ten and a half pence and were pleased with our purchase and went home.

My sister was very bothered about the poor man running the shop and that we had beaten him down in price; she really was sorry and concerned for him.

Anyway, our treasured butter dish was duly presented to our mother on her birthday and was well received and put into service for the birthday tea. During this she drew our uncle's attention to the dish and it was duly admired by all. But this was not enough for me as it had cost us a ruinous amount of money and I interjected by saying: "It was very expensive and cost us ten and a half pence".

At this juncture I thought the assembled company would have been impressed, but no! Instead, they roared with laughter for what seemed like a long time. By contrast, I saw nothing funny and simply wondered what I had done to cause such a strange reaction. Again, I was mystified about adult behaviour.

Other memories from those years include being fascinated by watching bumble bees in the garden forcing their way into

Antirrhinum blossoms and I was so intrigued by this that one day I decided to take hold of one. I had the shock of my life and, although I always was a noisy child, on this occasion the pain of the sting exacerbated the noise and quickly brought mother to my side to comfort me.

I used to play in the garden a lot and frequently heard my mother calling me or thought I did. Many a time I responded and went into the house to ask what she wanted only to be told that she had not called me. This kept happening and I began to wonder if there was telepathy between us; this awareness never left me.

On the other hand, it might have been childhood imagination as I could tell you the story about how I *saw* an echo and *saw* an alligator in our dustbin. I recounted this to the rest of the family but all I received was laughter. Confused again.

I think that being laughed at so often made me determined to get on in life so that people would no longer ridicule me.

(Author's note for this 2023 edition of my grandfather's autobiography: One old penny, 1d, was, as mentioned above, equivalent to $1/240^{th}$ of a £. In current value terms one old penny today can sell on the collectors' market for over £200.)

Chapter 2

School

When I was aged six my parents sent me to a small private school nearby. Having been told frequently at home that I was "very lazy" I was delighted to be able to run home at lunchtime after my first session in the school and to announce triumphally that I could do "pot hooks and hangers". Alas, I have absolutely no recollection of what this entailed.

Not long after this, I was sent to another private school about a mile away. I have no memory of making progress, but I clearly recall being regularly held back for detention. The school was run by a person I can only call the Old Dame. Again, I have scant memory of learning anything, but I managed just once to secure an apology from her. It is a simple story.

This lady was always adorned with a huge shawl and, so attired, she would wander through the classroom with the shawl swishing from side to side. Whilst I had no objection to this, I certainly did not appreciate her shawl being flicked into one of my eyes, causing me great pain. Strangely for me, this time I did not scream the house down and tried to be stoic. However, I could not prevent tears from pouring out of the affected eye and down my face which, in due course the Old Dame noticed. She came to me and asked how I was and, having explained the occurrence, she said that she was very sorry. On reflection, I do not think she was half as sorry I was. I thought she was thinking that I should have kept my eye out of the way of her shawl.

Times were quite hard then but at Christmas the school would hold a tea party for all the children at which, after a period of play, we were given our party tea, with extra jam, buns, and cakes and, in addition, a great luxury of a *quarter* of an orange. I thought only rich people could afford oranges and then they only had half of one at any one time whereas "ordinary" people like us were worthy of just a quarter. However, by cunning, I received some compensation for having my eye flicked with a shawl by being given a half orange myself. But little boys can be greedy, and I am sure I was one and had probably begged for the extra orange segments.

From that era, I recall many of my parents' friends suffering from gout; it was a common complaint then and probably reflected the meagre diet most people had. Today people are generally aware of the need to exercise, consume more fruit and vegetables and limit the amount of alcohol consumed but when I was very young this was not well known and above all, most people could not afford to improve their diet anyway.

The other common complaints were bilious attacks, i.e. headache, abdominal pain, constipation, et al. Today one rarely hears of the condition and the reason for this change is, likewise, probably the improved diet and exercise now enjoyed by much of the population.

After a while I was sent to another school run by yet another Old Dame. She was of middle age and possessed forbidding looks and reminded me of an elderly lioness. Her name was Hubbra, or similar, and, of course, we called her Old Mother Hubbard.

She was a terror for those who were afraid of her or whom she did not like. However, for some reason she seemed to like me, and it was soon clear that I was one of her favourites which I found embarrassing in that she plied me with jam and cake whilst denying her school boarders such pleasures. I found this awkward, and it perturbed me.

It was at this school that I started a school newspaper, having been encouraged by reading *The Boys' Own Paper,* a periodical of the time. I was greatly encouraged by Old Mother Hubbard and in due course, and with much credit from her, my newspaper was posted on the school notice board and acclaimed by her in a speech to the school in which she also warned that it should not be damaged in any way.

Alas, the school newspaper was found the next day defaced beyond recognition. Perhaps being a favourite of Old Mother Hubbard, and the recipient of special favours, had not endeared me to other boys at the school.

Old Mother Hubbard was wrathful at seeing the damage to my creation, but on the other hand I was pleased by the outcome and saw it as sufficient excuse for not producing any more school newspapers. The project had persuaded me that it was not something I enjoyed. That was the end of my first attempt at editing and publishing and I had no thought then of ever doing so again. (How wrong this proved to be!)

However, it was at this school that I found that I had begun to develop a gift for elocution. In fact, it seemed to come naturally, and reciting heroic poetry was my favourite.

At this juncture, when I was about 9 years old, Old Mother Hubbard advised my parents that I was gifted and talented but, being cynical, this may have been in part a promotion by the school to ensure that I was kept on as a pupil. Anyway, they entered me in a public recitation competition to be held in a newly built Presbyterian Church seating about 1,000. (My father was involved with this church as an Elder, having by now left the Baptists.)

It was at this new church that I was entered into the recitation competition, and I was to compete with older boys who had already won many prizes at other events.

Understandably, I felt dwarfed by them, in more senses than one, as they were all much taller than me.

The fateful evening arrived. There were two brothers competing against me, as well as some others, and the two brothers were expected to sweep the board. I thought I'd give it my best effort but, in my mind, I already saw either of them as the potential winner. I was more convinced of this outcome when I made a small error in the last verse of my performance whereas the reciting by the two other boys seemed splendid to me.

After their deliberation, the judges came back, and I thought they would flay me alive, but they said nothing. They duly criticised the other competitors and praised a few but did not even trouble to criticise me. This was worse than I had anticipated as I had hoped that at least I night have received "a mention" even though I did not expect a prize.

Then, when I thought the head judge was finished with his criticisms and comments, he said: "Therefore we award the first prize to Henry Hamblin". I was indeed surprised!

At this announcement the members of the audience were ecstatic; they clapped, some patted me on the back, and they all kept clapping and smiling. I could not understand it at all and thought there must have been a mistake. I went home a very puzzled little boy thinking that all the people at the event had suddenly become very silly.

Another abiding memory of this first recitation in the new Congregational church is of the noise made by the audience as they stood up at the end of the event. The seat varnish in the church was barely dry and as people stood up the result was a sound like tearing calico as each person unstuck themselves from the pews. I do not recall any clothing being damaged, but the noise it made is still in my memory!

After this first event I was called upon to recite at events for miles around, which meant travelling by pony and trap and often with a late return home on dark lanes and, if it was bad weather and raining and impossible to see enough to guide the horse, we were saved by the horse, which knew its way home. This was just as well as we had no real lights to help us.

I recall this incident, now that I look back over sixty years, and can see the parallel between that ride and our journey through life. On that dark night I sat with the horse's reins in my hands whilst sitting on the bench of the trap but was incapable of guiding the horse as I was unable to see the road in the dark. Life seems to be very much like that.

My analogy is, we cannot see where we are going; the road is unknown to us; there are deep ditches on either side; we do not always even know where we are going, or what the purpose of life is. All we know is that, to us, ours is an unknown journey along which we are obliged to travel propelled by time, which is remorseless. Instead of having strong headlights to show us the safe way, we have two flickering candle lamps. To my mind, they represent faith and hope. Even when these lamps are almost extinguished by the strong wind of temptation, we must continue the journey having trust that we are on the right path.

Although the way ahead in life may not be clear, we can completely trust God who alone knows the way. I have learnt in my long life that there is a power out there and an intelligence that can show us this way if only we allow it to. Above all there is love; for God and Jesus represent love in its widest sense. As with the horse, I had to trust its ability to guide us along a road which was unknown to me, and which was not visible because of the darkness. In life we have no option other than to trust God and His intelligence which surrounds us all and allows the clock of life to sweep us along.

My days of reciting came to an end as I got tired of it and of all the fuss that was made of me and eventually put my foot down and said: "no more". And I never did, as a child, recite again, and seldom in later life.

Eventually, the time came to leave that school; I had been well treated whilst there and it was my own fault that I learnt very little. When I left, which I did with some regret, the Head, Old Mother Hubbard, wrote these words on my Report: "Conduct, gentlemanly but talkative!" It was very kind of her to use the word "gentlemanly", but I do not think I deserved it, although I certainly deserved the other part – "talkative".

Next, I went to another private school which called itself a Commercial College, but it was much the same as other schools. The only things I can recall doing there were illuminated addresses and copperplate writing. I kept some of my work and wonder now how I ever created it as my writing today is far from "copperplate".

Finally, I went to an endowed Public School (which for the reader unfamiliar with the British tradition is a fee-paying private school). All the teaching staff were university graduates with degrees. However, it grieves me to admit that I learnt less at this school than at any of the others. Perhaps my mother had been correct to nickname me "Henry the Lazy".

I cannot condone my laziness knowing of the sacrifices my parents made to send me to this better school. I look back on this period of my life with shame.

I left school at age 15 with barely any useful education. It was entirely my fault that I did not do better.

However, during the latter years of my schooling, I had been plagued with many illnesses and when I was 15, I went into a marked decline in health, which contributed to my leaving school.

After leaving school I then went to a Technical College, but I lacked the required knowledge of mathematics or of much else. Why I was accepted I do not know, and my lack of general knowledge and my dreadful handwriting was hardly a good foundation for any technical training; but I went, and this will be the next chapter.

Finally, this chapter would be incomplete if I failed to mention religion. Looking back on my school years, I cannot remember receiving religious instruction although I am sure we would have had scripture lessons (or Divinity as it was often called then) but I have no recollection of this. From my experience, it does not follow that those who achieve high marks in these studies were any better people than those who finished at the bottom of the class; indeed, the reverse can often be the case.

It was, however, at Sunday School that we received most religious instruction, although we also had plenty of it at home. As soon as I could read, I was given children's books telling in simple words the main stories of the Bible and especially those of the Old Testament. My favourite story was about Joseph, and I revelled in it as it was about one young boy, demeaned by his older brothers, sold into slavery and without prospects, who makes good despite everything to become one of the most successful people in the country. To me it was inspirational.

However, the Devil gets in everywhere and even into the most religious families; he certainly got into ours!

Even if a religious background does not thwart the Devil, it does give the basic armoury to counter sin and my earlier life was certainly a sinful one, not because of my early upbringing, but in spite of it.

Many a time I have thanked God for the great privilege of having had a Christian home and upbringing together with the support of my parents' prayers. But for this restraining influence I could have been lost utterly. My belief is that the prayers of parents are not lost and can bear fruit even after a long time and in some cases after they have died.

No prayer is ever lost and, whenever we turn to God on behalf of another person, a blessing is created which multiplies throughout eternity.

This is my experience and my conviction.

The Divine way is to trust in God and to find His peace, first. After which the healing of the whole situation follows, as day follows night.

The Antidote for Worry.

HT Hamblin

Chapter 3

Technical School

I arrived at the Technical School one Monday morning not quite knowing what to expect and found that I was to work at a bench from 9am until 1pm and again from 2 to 5pm. In addition, on some evenings we had to attend lectures covering technical theory and draughtsmanship. It was a complete change of lifestyle but, for once, I was eager to learn.

Between 1pm and 2pm we had lunch and ate the food we had brought with us. The food I took was clearly not satisfactory. A jam turnover made of white flower was no fit food for a teenager working 7 to 9 hours a day with 3 hours travelling and walking in addition; I soon found myself becoming very tired. Moreover, when I returned home in the evening my dinner was a warmed-up meal consisting of twice-cooked food with re-warmed tea to go with it. In no time at all my health began to fail again.

Recognising the problem, my parents decided that they would have to spare 6 pence a day (old money) for me to eat a decent lunch. Several of us found a pleasant vegetarian restaurant in nearby Aldersgate Street, where downstairs the menu was à la carte and could cost a shilling (5p) each, whereas upstairs we boys could have 3 courses for 6 pence (2.5p). This was our opportunity. We chose the most filling and satisfying foods on the menu and each meal was a "blowout", which became all too obvious as we rushed back to the Technical School for the afternoon session.

Despite the disadvantages of this mode of feeding, I must have thrived on it as my health problems disappeared.

The only alternative we found for our 6 pence lunch was a "good pull-up for drivers" place where for 6 pence you could have a very thin slice of meat and 2 vegetables. It was poorly prepared, and I wondered how their regular diners could survive on it as they worked long hours driving their horses and carts around London.

At the Technical School I proved to be a satisfactory student, but there were many who were much better than me. However, the skills and knowledge I acquired there stood me in good stead in future years, as will become clear in later chapters (Chapter 5 onwards). On the theory side I managed to scrape through but had to do much work at home such as advanced arithmetic and basic algebra. However, technical drawing was more in my line, and I did well at it. Overall, I was middle of the road.

We were visited several times by senior members of the Institute Council who would assess our work and offer advice. What remains in my memory is the emphasis they placed on our training, saying that it would be of the greatest value in later life whether we were to be engaged in light or heavy engineering. For anyone following a scientific career, the training of eye and hand would prove to be of immense value. I imagined, then, that I would follow a life using tools and gauges, but little thought that one day the only tool I would be using would be a pen or pencil for my writing work. How inscrutable life is!

I took my weaknesses and lack of application with me to the Technical Institute and my report at the end was that I worked "by fits and starts". Sometimes I was most industrious and at others I was the worst of slackers and up to all sorts of wrongdoing. But I completed the course successfully although, clearly, I could have done better with more application, concentration, and perseverance.

My parents did not think I would succeed at anything. If they had known what I was to achieve in my life, they would have been incredulous.

They had good reason to take this view as I won no prizes at school except for drawing and elocution and my school reports were depressing in the extreme. I would start new things with enthusiasm but then lose interest and never finish them; I had many good ideas but failed to take the work to a conclusion. It was said to me often: "The idea was all right, if only you had kept on with it".

Interestingly, my mother once took me to a Phrenologist to "have my bumps felt" so that my likely capabilities could be revealed. He felt my head and deduced that I could become a good draughtsman, engineer, scientific instrument maker, etc, which was encouraging. But then he suddenly stopped feeling my head and exclaimed: "But he is totally lacking in perseverance and will start things and never finish them; he will never succeed unless he learns to persevere".

He was quite correct, and that was my failing. By contrast my brother always completed whatever task he set out to achieve, whereas I rarely finished anything. One day, I recall my brother saying with some disgust: "You are a perfect messer... you mess about and what do you have to show for it? Why, nothing". He was quite correct and, clearly, I was doomed to be a failure in life.

My mother, God bless her, tried to reclaim me, and meant well and was earnest in her endeavours but had no knowledge of how the human mind functions. She thought the best approach was to remind me frequently of my failings which proved to be most unhelpful. With the benefit of hindsight, encouragement would have been more beneficial.

Alas, mother did not know of this and, to make matters worse, she found a Biblical text (Genesis 49.4) and took it from its context and bombarded me with it: *"Unstable as water, thou shalt not excel"*. (This had been her regular quotation from my earliest years.)

It was bad enough to be unstable, and lacking in application and perseverance but, when added to the burden of adverse suggestion, my difficulties became formidable. The often-quoted Biblical text discouraged and rendered impotent a perfectly normal boy. Unfortunately, the wonderful power of suggestion was not known at the time, but its discovery was to be a cornerstone of my life's work in later years.

Although my parents, brother and sister believed that I could never make a success of life, God had other ideas; He was preparing to use the foolish and weak.

My great regret is that my mother did not live long enough to see me confound all the family fears and forebodings about me which, by the Grace of God, were refuted.

I graduated from the Technical Institute with some regret – I had no ideas about my future.

But these early years reveal a clue. When I was young, I read avidly. The first publication I became absorbed in was *The Boys' Own Paper*, which my father bought for four and a half pence (old money) from a discount shop; every penny was precious in those days. My brother, being the eldest, had the first reading. Then it was my sister's turn and finally mine. I became absorbed with reading and included a wide range of titles and particularly biographies about the great men who helped found the United States of America. I loved inspirational stories about adventurers and explorers. They all put ideas into my head.

Then there were religious magazines and books for children, all of which I enjoyed. I feel sure that I must have read books about Jesus for children, but I cannot remember these clearly.

Whereas my father was content to be a cog in someone else's machine, it was my mother who had a sense of enterprise. It was she who gave me the books about boys from a poor background who had risen to become great men. These varied books inspired me and showed me that a poor boy could achieve great things in life and, if those about whom these books were written could do so, then so could I.

But the family, and all those around us in our community, were in a cage of poverty. My brother, who had done well at school and was knowledgeable and mentally bright, was a clerk in the City of London earning eighteen shillings a week (90 pence in decimal currency). That was the standard wage for clerks in those days and for long after; these amounts equated to between £40 and £50 per annum. What were my brother's prospects? There were none.

In addition, all of us went in fear of unemployment. It was a nightmare that bothered me for many years; I just had to get myself out of the rut.

I grew up with a determination to change all this as this book will explain. But first there were difficult days ahead...

If we would only trust God more and make greater and more daring ventures in faith, then it would not be necessary for us to be driven by life's experiences to the end of our tether.

God's Sustaining Grace

HT Hamblin

Chapter 4

A Disturbing Experience

At the age of sixteen, I was overwhelmed by melancholy. It was as though all the sadness of all who ever lived was placed upon me and I felt all the anguish of countless millions searing and breaking my heart. From this experience I felt I could understand, very imperfectly of course, what Jesus suffered in Gethsemane when, as the Bible tells us, all the sorrows of the world were willingly borne by Him.

This went on for many months until I had a tremendous experience when, without any warning, I suddenly became aware that the Henry Thomas Hamblin I had thought myself to be was not me! In a curious way I realised this was not my true identity. This was very disturbing. Strange too.

My thoughts were "Who am I and what am I doing here?"

This was, in effect, the "cracking of my ego shell" and at times I was terrified.

Naturally I went to my parents, who were good Christian people, thinking that they would be able to help me. When I exclaimed "Who am I and what am I doing here?" they were clearly both puzzled and distressed. They answered: "Why, you are Henry Thomas Hamblin, of course". I responded: "Yes, but who am I *really*?" in response to which they looked distressed.

Not being content with their advice, I went to our church minister and asked him the same question, thinking that he, being a shepherd of souls, would surely be able to help answer my question: "Who am I and what am I doing here?" but he was as much in the dark as my parents. He said he had never had such a feeling himself, which he called an awakening, and neither had he come across such an experience in others. He tried by persuasion to push me back into my ego-shell again. But it was too late; something very profound had happened to me and there could be no going back.

Being concerned about the experience, I asked other people, but they too could not help and instead looked at me as though I was out of my mind. I gave up the request as far as human beings were concerned.

I suppose, looking back at it over more than half a century later, that the only way I could have expressed myself more clearly would have been to say: "I do not know who I am, but I am what I am".

It reads very tamely now but, at the time of the event, it was an alarming one for a lad of only 16 years to endure. I have never met anyone else who has had a similar experience, but I am sure there will be many.

I wrote of this experience many years later in *The Science of Thought Review* of September 1943 and heard back from a small number of other people who had had similar experiences. One of them came to see me, a Salvation Army Officer. He told me that when he was troubled by the experience, he used an *I AM* affirmation which he found lifted him up, as he termed it, "to be one with the gods". My advice, however, to those of us affected by a similar condition is to hide these things in their hearts and share their concerns with God in prayer.

We may discover, in the same way that St Paul had been after he had been caught up in the Third Heaven, or Paradise as some accounts use, with a feeling of illimitable power and harmony with God.

It was strange that this disturbing experience came to one so young and that it should have come unsought.

Now, over 50 years later, I have learnt that in India there are teachers who specialise in this subject and who teach the pupil the nature of the *I*. They teach one to get behind the ego-hood into the real Self. In this country I know of no such teaching by the churches.

Thus, I found myself alone with no one to help and thought I would try to forget all about it and attempted to do so but failed fully to expunge the memory. But I had learnt from the experience that my inner self, my soul, the *I* in me, was deathless, diseaseless and eternal. This was a life-changing experience for one so young; I knew that the eternal Truth was in God and that this was true also of my inner self.

Having had such an experience, I could not forget that "I am what I am", and not the external person known to the world as Henry Thomas Hamblin. Had it proved possible to receive help and encouragement at this juncture from someone who was enlightened in such matters, I might have blossomed out into a fully awakened soul. Alas, there was no one I knew who understood anything about spiritual matters and I was left with no option other than to try and revert to my old self which I knew before I had this experience.

In this I was only partially successful, and it proved impossible to forget the events I had been through, although I tried hard to do so. I was advised to revert to being "normal", the same as other boys, and to be interested in material things. I followed this advice and attempted to forget all about the experiences I had endured but failed to do so.

This experience had revealed to me the eternal nature of the soul and I realised then that my soul was eternal, without death and disease. A strange realisation for a young person.

However, I became so "normal" (some friends called it "sane") that a year or so later I was approached by the local Church Fathers with a view to joining the Church and becoming a communicant. I agreed.

Naturally, this required some preparation, which I found a rather tiresome business. It commenced with some solemn-faced visitors coming to see me and asking all sorts of doctrinal questions. I must admit to not particularly warming to these people. They reminded me of the type of person employed by undertakers to carry coffins and were solemn faced but certainly not mute. I only wished they had been mute because they talked far too much for my liking.

They informed me that to become a member of the Baptist Church I had to be baptised, which meant total immersion. The tradition was adult baptism rather than child christening as in most other denominations. The Baptist rule is that baptism must be an adult profession of faith.

The Baptism was held one evening with the church being crowded and the galleries, which afforded the best view of the ceremony, being overcrowded. I thought of the Arena at Rome, albeit on a small scale; perhaps it was the same love of spectacle they sought.

It was a solemn Service. The platform in front of the pulpit had been removed to reveal a small pool filled with water. The minister, appropriately robed for the occasion, explained to the congregation that the Church practised adult Baptism with total immersion. He reminded everyone that the Baptist Church only baptised those old enough to have a real understanding of the Christian faith and total immersion follows the example of Jesus and the early church which baptised this way.

We "candidates", as we were called, were arranged on either side of the pool, ladies on one side and men on the other.

With due solemnity, the minister stepped into the water and each candidate was immersed into it and then raised up by the minister.

And then it was my turn. It was a solemn moment for me and one which I had dreaded for some time. Down into the water I stepped and began to wade towards the minister. As I did so, I became conscious of a great and joyous spiritual sensation.

In those days I could never be called a very happy person but now I experienced something that was at a level higher than normal happiness. I suddenly felt lifted with what I can only call Heavenly Joy. I had never felt like it before. It made me feel perfectly at home and at peace.

The baptism was dramatic. The minister grasped me firmly by the shoulders and, in a strong clear voice, spoke my name and said: "on profession of your faith in the Lord Jesus Christ, I baptise you in the name of the Father, Son, and the Holy Ghost". Then he immersed me completely and raised me out of the water again. It was extraordinary and I was aware of a glorious feeling that I can only describe as a Spiritual Presence, which from now on I will now simply refer to as the Presence.

I made my way out of the pool and into the dressing room.

There is no doubt in my mind that the rite of Baptism is a true Sacrament which is attended by some great Presence.

However, the Presence I mention is not limited to the full immersion type of baptism as I have experienced the same all-powerful feeling at infant baptisms.

I remember one such service. The people around me were very pleasant but of a worldly disposition and I felt alone, and it did not seem possible to pray in such circumstances. However, I experienced a pleasing surprise when the actual baptism took place becoming immediately aware of a powerful Presence embracing us all. I felt somehow lifted above time and space and into a glorious feeling of unity with the children of God.

I deduced that God was clearly present at all Baptisms regardless of whether those who perform the rite are aware of it.

After my baptism the next ordeal, as I saw it, was to be received into the Church fully so that I could partake in the other great sacrament, the Lord's Supper, commonly called the Communion Service. I expected it to be attended by the Presence I had so clearly felt at the Baptism ceremony. Alas, I was disappointed and did not have the same feeling in any way.

Naturally, I thought that I must have failed in some aspect and searched my conscience for a sin of omission on my part which might have accounted for the failure. But I could find nothing and could not explain why I felt the Presence at the Baptism but not at the Communion Service. This troubled me.

Therefore, I spoke to some who had been regular communicants for years and asked why the Presence had not been there. They were unable to help me in any way and clearly indicated that they did not know what I was talking about. To them the Communion Service was just another event they felt obliged to attend but they had no idea what I meant by the term I used of the Presence.

I spoke to others who had been baptised and some said that they too had experienced a great uplifting feeling at their Baptism but had experienced no such uplift at a Communion Service.

Later, I eavesdropped on my father when he was telling some friends that his greatest disappointment was the Communion Service. His experience had been like mine; a great realisation of the Presence during baptism but no such feeling at the Communion Service.

I pondered this.

I thought that it might be that these friends missed the meaning of the Communion Service in that they followed the Apostle Paul's philosophy that it was simply a remembrance of the sufferings and death of Jesus. However, this is not what Jesus said. If we read the account of the last supper, we see that it was symbolic of what takes place within, when the soul feeds on the Divine, the body of Christ, and drinks the Life of God, the blood of Christ. I do not know, of course, but I surmise that, had my friends realised this, they might have found the Presence not far from them at the service.

Enough on spiritual matters for the moment and I will move on to another series of events which, although challenging, helped equip me for my future life. Let me explain.

At around the time of my Baptism and first Communion, I was inveigled into joining a Young Men's Debating Society. It did not seem very important at the time but, looking back, it was one of the best things I ever did.

Unlike the title of this chapter, it was not disturbing.

When I tried to speak to an audience for the first time it was gruelling. I was a sensitive young man and had no experience of being ridiculed and was totally unprepared for the hard blows which everyone, who speaks in public debate, receives. I used to go home crushed and discouraged and told myself that I would never do this sort of thing again.

Of course, I did do it again!

By the time the next meeting came round I was ready to enter the fray and knew what to expect. I spoke on a wide variety of subjects, whether I knew anything about them or not, and quickly learnt to think on my feet and, to a limited extent, to argue with confidence.

I believe I became a competent speaker, although I never became a powerful debater. To my annoyance, I would often think of the things I should have said and the ripostes I should have used, but only when I was on my way home!

There was one occasion when I knew more about the subject under debate than anyone else and let myself go. The Chairman was generous and allowed me to exceed my time. I went home afterwards feeling very pleased with myself but was less than pleased when the local newspaper reported my effort as a Humorous Oration.

Despite disappointments and failures, I made real progress, and what I learnt in the rough and tumble of the training I received served me well in later life.

Only once did I achieve real success or even a triumph. This was in an essay competition. We competitors were given a subject to address a week before the next debate and were expected to read our respective papers at the following meeting. I do not remember what my subject was, but I can remember treating it in a humorous, not to say hilarious, fashion. At the same time, I took the opportunity to get my own back on some other members who had chosen to give me a rough passage on the debating floor. Now was the time, I thought, to get even and make them sit up just as they had done to me earlier.

I succeeded.

In the words of the head of the judges I used my "genius for sarcasm" to good effect. I had no thought that I might win the prize and let myself be forceful and confident in my delivery and thoroughly enjoyed myself. As I read my paper, I could feel the audience responding and, by the time I had completed reading it, they were highly responsive and enthusiastic.

It soon became evident that there were only two of us in the running on this occasion and, to my surprise, I was one of them. The other person was the minister's grandson who was just down from university. He was clearly a well-educated person with a "highbrow" literary style and therefore his paper was quite different to mine. The reaction from the audience showed that it did not appeal to them very much, but I was sure it would have appealed to the judges.

In the end the prize went to this other man with his excellent literary style and for the content of his paper. But this clearly did not please the bulk of the audience who received the verdict coolly. The head of the judges had more to say about my paper than about that of my competitor and he warned me against what he called "my brilliance" especially in sarcasm and satire. He went on to say that it was so forthright that it could get me into trouble one day if I did not curb myself.

But then one of the other judges stood up and said he wished to disassociate himself from nearly all the criticism just offered by the head of the judges. Amazingly, he went on to say that he thoroughly disagreed with the verdict and that he would have awarded the prize to me without hesitation. Then he gave his reasons, but I do not recall exactly what they were; however, his remarks were applauded by the audience. It was a memorable experience for me, even though I did not win the prize.

Whilst the other man's paper was far superior to mine, particularly in its literary style, mine was more popular with the audience because, I believe, it was more forthright than the other and my delivery kept them laughing nearly all the time. I suspect that I jolted them out of their normal "comfort zone" as my remarks were to some extent at their expense.

So why have I included this story in this little book, as it is only about a relatively small experience?

There are several reasons. First a Debating Society is a good thing for a young man to engage in as it offers benefits almost as useful as a formal education. Second it gives an opportunity for an almost uneducated youth, like me, to come close to beating a man with a university education. And third, this partial success in writing a paper was, with hindsight, a straw blowing in the wind which revealed the way my later life would evolve.

Little did I think then that I would eventually become a writer, albeit of sorts!

On looking back, I regard the incident of the Debating Society as one of the most important events of my early life. Until this juncture, I had been told again and again that because I failed at school, had won no prizes, and had passed no examinations, I could never succeed in life. I was told that only those who win prizes and scholarships could succeed. Because of this I was inclined to believe that I would, indeed, not succeed and knew well that I had not embraced the challenges life had already given me.

However, the Essay Competition exploded this idea completely and I realised that when it came to appealing to ordinary people, punch and personality were far more powerful weapons than just education and the niceties of literary style. I was emboldened as I could see that there was a place for me in the great scheme of things and that I could indeed succeed where better educated people might not.

The experience was to prove pivotal, but not for many years.

Life must be a continual winning through, both in things practical and outward, and in things spiritual and inward.

The Open Door

HT Hamblin

Chapter 5

Difficult Years

With the Disturbing Experience chapter behind us it is time to move back to the Technical Institute with which I had been involved throughout the period of these experiences. We are in the year 1890.

The time arrived when I had completed the course at the Technical Institute and the next step was to find employment as an "improver". This would be a halfway step between the Institute and fully qualified work. *(Author's note: The concept of the "improver" was to try to bridge the gap between the social classes in late Victorian society.)*

The Institute course, although good and efficient in its delivery, was no substitute for the traditional apprenticeship. The latter, once trained, not only knew their work thoroughly but were quick and efficient in executing it. Whereas an "improver" was little more than a student who had studied the theory and could execute good work given time but was generally inexperienced and slow compared to a trained apprentice.

Thus, potential employers either did not want us "improvers" at all or, if they were willing to give us a trial, they would only pay us a pittance.

Eventually I secured my first job and was paid ten shillings a week (50p in decimal currency) out of which I had to pay railway fares and other expenses. I thought back to all my expenses in training and concluded that my work was far worse than being a clerk, which was the role my brother was employed in and being paid eighteen shillings a week (90p).

Wages were very low in those days, and work was hard to find. The streets of London swarmed with dirty, half-starved children who were barefooted even in the coldest weather. They were filthy themselves beyond description and were wearing rags which were even filthier, if that were possible.

Food was scarce and I remember watching a greengrocer throwing rotting plums out of the front of his shop into the muddy road. Instantly, and seemingly from nowhere, sprang several barefooted, rag-clad children, who fought and scrambled for the unexpected prizes now lying in the road. That the fruit was rotten and covered in mud did not seem to matter to these poor famished children.

Also, it was common in those days to see groups of starving men walking along the streets and saying in hoarse voices: "We have no work to do; we are poor honest working men". I could see that they really were in bad shape as their faces were wasted and their eyes wild-looking, revealing that they were terrified of their situation.

Once I remember seeing a starving man with a new loaf of white bread which he had probably "acquired" when the shop owner's back was turned. He was hurrying along as fast as his weakened body would allow, tearing at the softer parts of the loaf with dirty talon-like fingers. His face was sunken, his eyes had a wolfish look in them, and his clothes were in rags. It was a most disturbing sight and enough to move the gods and yet no one seemed to take any notice. That was one of the terrible things about those days, the complete indifference of most people to the sufferings of the poor.

I look back on that period and cannot help thinking of the workless and the starving, the children searching the gutters for scraps of food and the ten shillings a week I received for 6 days' skilled work, and I wonder why they are often spoken of as "the good old days".

At about this time, my parents became interested in Band of Hope meetings which were held at what was known as a Board School. The Band of Hope was a temperance organisation for working class children. These Board Schools were the first attempts in the country to introduce a state school system with an aim of producing some degree of standardisation whilst leaving the running of them to local management. Attendance could be from age 5 to 13 years.

They decided to visit such a school and unfortunately, they insisted I go with them. I wish I hadn't.

I shall never forget the experience, especially the awful smells. The children stank and some were worse than others. Some were not even house-clean. I found it a disturbing and unpleasant experience; indeed, it was painful. I shall never forget the stenches and can still, in my mind, smell them today over 50 years later. These are not nice words to write, but I need to use them to illustrate the level of deprivation in our society in those years.

Another recollection from this visit was meeting the Board School caretaker, who was clearly a decent man, and the thing which is relevant to my own story is that he welcomed us with the words "Oh you have *came* then". His remark puzzled me, and I could not work out why he used the word *came* instead of *come*.

This was when I discovered that I am a very literal person and realised that I take written or spoken words at face value. Many years later, when I was working with *The Science of Thought Review*, I often found that I could not decipher individual words in handwritten letters sent to me as editor and had to ask a member of my staff to do so. Clearly, I have never had the ability to scan a whole sentence for its meaning.

Amusingly, this tendency to be literal once created a minor issue for me whilst I was starting out in life. I had been invited to a tea party given by our local baker and, during a lull in the party, I was taken into the shop by the baker's daughter, where I saw fancy pastry and every kind of bun and cake. The daughter told me to help myself and have whatever I liked.

When she returned, I saw a look of horror in her face when she realised that I had seriously depleted the stock of cakes and buns in the shop. She explained: "When I said help yourself, I did not mean that you were to eat as much as you could". I had taken her word of "whatever" literally. I hope I learnt a lesson!

But I digress and must return to the Band of Hope and Board Schools and The Pledge. By signing The Pledge, the person doing so promised to forgo consuming alcohol in any form.

My father and mother were, in my view, totally unfitted to their self-appointed task. They told the children that if they signed the Pledge, they would become clean and happy, well-fed, and well-clothed. It was a wonderful idea, or would have been, had it been true.

The whole idea of these meetings was to get as many children as possible to sign and thus require them to abstain from the consumption of intoxicating liquors. Nothing was said about how long they had to keep to The Pledge. For poor children living in the utmost squalor in poverty-stricken homes, whose parents were often inebriated, and where the breadwinner was on poverty pay, I saw no prospect of them being able to keep The Pledge.

Despite the best efforts of my parents, the Band of Hope meetings degenerated into near chaos with the children in control. The children were cajoled, implored, commanded to be quiet, and to pay attention, if even for a moment, but uproar would break out again together with violence.

It was utter pandemonium.

In vain my parents struggled but did not prevail as Father lacked force and Mother was diminutive, with her height of 4 feet and 10 inches. Also, she had a weak voice and had never had any teaching experience.

But it was a noble idea, and I became steeped in the Band of

Hope work and was a supporter of the total abstinence movement and had signed The Pledge myself. But, at the time, I was still living at home and there was no temptation to ignore my undertaking. This restraint fell away later, as I will reveal shortly.

As for Board Schools, they at least had the benefit of being the beginning of a proper national education system but the absolute poverty of the homes the children came from was deeply distressing. I wondered what became of the poor children despite their signing of The Pledge. They would surely have gone home to utter poverty and dreadful living conditions with minimal parenting.

I had the benefit of coming from a loving family with full parental support and a clear code of Christian behaviour, whereas the children I saw at the Board School were at a huge disadvantage. I deduce that they probably had little moral compass to follow and that our attempt to get them to sign The Pledge and abstain from alcohol might not have meant much. On the other hand, our efforts may have made them turn against drink; I just do not know.

I remained concerned about what I had experienced at the Board School, which was, incidentally, situated on what was then called Muddy Island. It was close to the track of the London, Brighton and South Coast Railway on the edge of a cutting that was prone to flooding; it was truly a dreadful place. I well remember one afternoon when an unusually violent thunderstorm accompanied by torrential rain struck the area, which caused huge floods on the railway and produced several feet of water which reached up to platform level. The Board School was flooded too, and I wondered what would be happening to the people affected, and especially to the children. Even in those early days I wondered why such things should be. Why was I fortunate to live in a comfortable house whilst the poor lived in hovels on land prone to flooding? This left me with a sense of injustice but, clearly, I was powerless to remedy the situation.

I tell this story to emphasise how dreadful life was for so many people in those late Victorian days. I reiterate my earlier remark questioning the phrase "the good old days". They were not.

Turning back to The Pledge, at home there was no temptation to go against it. At the time I lived the most austere life possible and then, as my life took me away from the restraints of home, I found myself in a phase of indulgence as a reaction to the strict life at home. I ignored The Pledge and went off the rails, as they say. But that story is in a later chapter.

Back to my work. I stuck with my job and more than earned my salary. I had been allocated a quiet workshop where I was free to do much as I liked, even to working on personal projects, which was permitted providing there was no delay to the completion of work I was doing for the firm.

On the floor above me in the building there was an artist who loved to say that he got "hung" at the Royal Academy every year. This may have been true, I just do not know, but he was principally a violin maker. He also liked singing, and whilst he was making violins, he used to sing in a loud voice. After he had stopped singing, or stopped for breath, I delighted in responding by singing from below in retaliation. Whereas he sang classical songs, I would respond with the latest popular ditty but would forget the words and the tune. There was silence from the room above when I stopped.

We only met occasionally, and this would be on the stairs. The artist-cum-violin maker would give me a quizzical look each time as though he would like to tell me about many things for my own good. But he was far too courteous ever to do so.

In addition to my workshop duties, I was required to visit the local bank for the firm and pay money in and to make business visits to prospective customers to which I would take valuable specimens of our work. And I did all this for just ten shillings (50p) a week.

However, this routine was not to last, as at that time influenza was rampant and it was a very virulent strain. Like others, I was far from immune and seemed to fall victim to every epidemic. As each epidemic swept London, down I went and was usually very badly affected. As soon as I was well enough, though, I'd get back to my workbench only to relapse again and then again. Life was certainly not easy.

My health became so uncertain that I left my job and, as my expenses had exceeded my remuneration, this was no loss financially. I tried to do some work at home but was unsuccessful. Moreover, where we lived was well out of the business district of London and, also, my own youthful appearance certainly worked against me as I was regarded by potential customers as inexperienced.

I needed to think of something else to do.

During this period, I was visited by some of my recent fellow students. One was by far the best and most skilled and quickest worker of them all. He told me he was self-employed and very busy and was able to earn 15 shillings a week (75p).

This depressed me. If our best student and quickest worker was able to earn only such a paltry sum, I felt we were all in some sort of cage with no possible way out. Everybody I knew who was in "our station in life" seemed to be similarly trapped in this cycle of low wages, poor prospects and, in too many cases, no prospects at all. And all the time there was a constant fear of unemployment.

I puzzled over the situation and could see no remedy. It was not merely a matter of education or lack of it as I knew men who were highly educated, and even able to speak several languages, who were trapped in unemployment or, at best, low-pay employment.

I thought that there must be some way out of this quagmire because I knew of young men, even poorer than I was, who had achieved great success in business despite the disadvantage of being born into an impoverished family.

I read and re-read the many inspirational books I had been given earlier including *From Log Cabin to White House, John Halifax Gentleman,* and others. From what I could ascertain from these books, the success of their heroes was due entirely to their powers of application, concentration, perseverance and determination, as well as other virtues and qualities. Alas, I knew that I was deficient in many of these and certainly did not qualify for my perseverance and sustained application. I knew that I could only work in "fits and starts" and the qualities I lacked were, as I saw them, staying power, finishing power, perseverance, and persistence.

I had a relative mountain to climb.

I knew that I lacked the determination and "grit" that so many successful people seemed to have and, deep down, I was conscious of my mother's repeated comment dragged out of the book of Genesis that I was unstable and could not excel. No wonder I found life difficult!

How much easier it would have been to have had an H.G. Wells time machine, and turned it forward, so that in 1891 I could have had one of my own books to read, in which I dealt with Positive Thinking, and which I started to produce from about 1920. What a difference it would have made to my life!

But of course, that was not possible and, as there were no books of the right kind available, I had no option open to me other than to find out the hard way by blundering along and learning from experience.

The outlook was very bleak as far as my future was concerned. I was earning practically nothing, had no prospect of earning more, work was hard to obtain, and nobody wanted to employ me. To cap it all, my health was erratic and generally poor.

My parents were deeply worried and could not afford to keep me in idleness; I was deeply worried too. I wanted not only to earn a living but to get on in life. And yet I lacked the vision, the determination, and the required application to achieve success. And all the time I felt dragged down by that dreadful quotation my mother kept giving me and which was always on my mind: "Unstable as water, thou shalt not excel."

Suggestion is a very powerful force, as is positive thinking and, little did I realise at the time, this was to be the focus of much of my later work in life. But I was not there yet.

Broken in health, considered too delicate to secure another job in London, the victim of misapplied suggestion, I still had deep determination to rise to the top. But there seemed to be no chance to achieve this as I was so ill-equipped.

And there was worse to follow, including my folly, sin, and wrongdoing, that I shall reveal in the following chapters.

However, you will be puzzled to know why I, as a young man spiritually awakened, and having been baptised and belonging to a church, could not follow in a path of decency and probity.

The fact of the matter was that I was a backslider. I had a difficult and strange temperament and seemed to be a saint at one moment and a devil at another. When I was trying to be a saint my one desire (while it lasted) was to be a saint; I had no desire to be otherwise. But then this phase would pass, and I would plunge into sin and become far worse than those who stayed in sin all the time. I was a human pendulum, swinging first to one extreme and then to the other. I had no idea where it would all end.

As I conclude this chapter, I must make it clear that I am not complaining about life and its challenges and about those I faced. Rather, I realise now that all life's experiences are necessary, and it is the way we deal with them which is important.

As I look back, I see God's hand in everything and recognise that Divine love has been with me always although I did not recognise it at the time. My later emergence from this dark tunnel has been entirely due to the grace of God. I can see now that all my life has been crowded with blessings and that most of my troubles and sufferings were due to my being out of harmony, or out of step, with the life that had been set out for me. The perfect life is the one in which Divine love and Wisdom are the key components.

I remember the Lord's guidance when praying: *"Thy Kingdom come, Thy Will be done; in earth as it is in Heaven"*. I should have remembered it in my earlier Difficult Years.

But at least I was now at home.

True prayer is… the lifting of the heart to the higher spiritual plane… it is finding the repose, peace, and harmony of the Inner Spiritual Reality.

Simple Talks on the Science of Thought

HT Hamblin

Chapter 6

I Leave Home

My health gradually improved from living at home, and I enjoyed being able to spend the larger part of my time in the open air. I had little to no work to do and my parents thought that I was not yet strong enough to seek fresh employment in London. At this juncture I was fortunate to be given a loan by my uncle sufficient for me to be able to buy a bicycle; it was what would now be called a "Penny Farthing" with a large 53-inch wheel at the front and a very small one at the rear. In those days they were called "ordinary" bicycles whilst the very latest bicycles, called "safety bicycles", were just appearing, having been first produced only a few years before in 1885.

I was able to repay my uncle's loan.

This new bicycle enabled me to make long trips into the country and I became one of many such riders who were regarded as being daring and brave for riding such machines. I was neither, but I did enjoy the freedom and the spice of adventure it added to my life. Undoubtedly this was made possible by my steadily improving health and, in turn, the bicycle rides also contributed to this.

But probably the greatest factor in bringing about my improved health was that I was eating better food by being at home although no one then, least of all my dear mother, knew anything about food values and a balanced diet.

The trigger for my breakdown in health occurred was when I was employed as an "improver" on ten shillings a week. In the part of London in which I was based for this work, there were no restaurants offering the likes of "three courses for sixpence" and I cannot remember ever having a meal away from my place of work and deduce that I must have relied on the food I took with me. My mother was a frugal person although, as I have already mentioned, she, in common with everybody else in those days, was not aware of food values and I am sure that I was starved of essential food elements. For example, in those days cheese was so cheap that it was almost given away and yet we in our household never ate it and it was certainly never in my sandwiches. If I had had a cheese sandwich every day, and green vegetables and tomatoes in season I would, most probably, have been well nourished. Moreover, I believe that the cost could well have been no more than the food my mother so kindly provided every day.

Just to make the point more strongly, cheese was so cheap then, almost as cheap as bread, and yet in the family we were only permitted to have a morsel, and this at night, just before going to bed. We had to eat a tremendous amount of bread to qualify for a morsel of cheese. My dear mother did not know of the vital necessity of protein food and certainly did not know that cheese contains a higher percentage of protein than almost any other food. In ignorance, we were fed on white flour pastry with jam in it.

I well remember my uncle taking me out in his "dog-cart", a light horse-drawn vehicle, and we travelled well into the country for some eight miles. In the late morning of this journey, we approached an inn, whereupon my uncle disappeared inside and then re-appeared bringing me a large glass of ginger beer and a great hunk of new bread containing a slab of cheese almost as thick as the bread. The cheese would have lasted us weeks at home, but I was expected to eat it all in a few minutes!

I ate all the bread, and as much of the cheese as I could, but managed only to nibble round the edges of the slab. The bulk remained. Not knowing what to do with the large chunk remaining I asked my uncle what I should do with it. I was shocked and amazed to be told "chuck it away, mate". To one who had been brought up in a home where every morsel and crumb was carefully conserved before being used, such a thing was unthinkable and I commented that this seemed a huge waste; he turned to me, smiling, and repeated his advice to "chuck it away".

Instead of throwing it away on to the muddy road, I leant out of the dog-cart and carefully dropped the cheese onto the grass verge, where I was sure a passing tramp would find it. Tramps swarmed the road in those days. They never had any work to do and lived on scraps of food they either found, purloined, or were given. Strangely they never seemed to be unhappy.

My parents and I decided that it would not be prudent for me to go back to London and that a better option would be to seek work in the open country where the environment would be more health-giving than in London. This idea was strongly supported by a friend of my parents, who argued that working in the country would be less of a strain on me and that life away from home would make a man of me. My parents were hesitant, but their friend was able to overcome their concerns, especially when he said that he had the ideal job for me in mind.

I took the post he advised and was off to East Anglia, some 120 miles away, to be employed at a wage which was sufficient to leave me with about ten shillings a week after paying all expenses such as board, lodging, washing, and mending etc.

This alone gave me a wonderful sense of freedom and security. For the first time in my life, I realised that I was truly self-supporting and no longer a burden on my parents. I would never need to trouble them for money again.

It was a lovely time of year when I arrived in East Anglia to a village near Norwich. It was early September and, after a summer with indifferent weather, we were now enjoying a spell of unbroken golden colour sunshine such as I had never seen before. At night the moonlight was so inspiring that it left me speechless and aroused emotions in me which I could not even start to describe or understand.

My new job saw me working long hours but, after work in the evenings, and often later at night, I took the opportunity to explore the countryside both on foot and on my penny-farthing bicycle. I had been told that the countryside was generally flat and that I need not worry about hills because there were none.

This was not strictly accurate, and I found this out the hard way in an accident that could easily have cost me my life. The story is simple; bicycles had very poor lights then and mine was no exception; there was enough light from the sky to see the outline of the road but insufficient to see any detail and my lamp would only show a yard ahead. This was to be my undoing.

I proceeded to ride into the darkness, not knowing where I was going, but able to follow the road, when I suddenly felt the machine falling away from me. I realised that I had encountered a very steep hill and that the only solution to my predicament would be to jump for it. I did this in less time than it will take you to read this. I was uninjured! I walked down the hill and retrieved my machine, which also was undamaged.

Before reversing my journey to return to my lodgings I went on down to the bottom of the hill and noted that there was a road running at right angles with a stone wall on the other side.

A narrow escape, I told myself.

When I got back to my lodgings, I mentioned the incident to my landlord, who said that either I was lucky or extremely agile because only recently an experienced local bicyclist ("cysiclist" as they were called in East Anglia in those days) had lost control on the same hill, hit the wall, and broken his neck.

I pondered my survival.

I wondered why the other man broke his neck while I did not even sprain an ankle. I thought that perhaps God might have some use for me after all. Or was it just luck?

Were our lives like acorns falling from a tree, some to be eaten by pigs, some to become crushed and broken, and only a few surviving to grow into oaks? The man whose neck had been broken was probably a much better man than I was; what had I done to be preserved?

Despite these thoughts, I could not help wondering if, in all the apparent hopelessness of my situation in life, there might be some sort of role for me. Could it be possible that, despite my weak character, my lack of education, and my lowly position in life, that I could ever rise out of the rut in which I found myself?

There seemed to be no way of escape, no opening into a more congenial life. I felt as though I was living in a blind alley with nothing to look forward to apart from labouring for someone else for the best years of my life and then to be discarded into the pool of the unemployed once I was too old to be able to work hard enough to justify my remuneration.

I looked around me. Was there *no* way out? I could not become a doctor, a dentist, a lawyer, or enter any of the professions because they were all closed to a youth from a poor background who had received little education.

I set to work trying to establish how I might escape.

What about becoming a church minister? I thought. I knew that I could become a preacher as I had earlier had a few sessions doing so which were well received by the congregation and I suspected that I had inherited some of my paternal grandfather's ability to preach. But I did not feel that I had a definite "call" to commit to such work. Anyway, the training period was too long for me to endure to qualify as a minister in the Nonconformist church and would be very poorly paid. It did not appeal strongly, but it could be a way out of my predicament, as there were always ways and means to be found to achieve this goal if the youth concerned possessed true ability and believed strongly that he had truly received a call from God to do such work. But I did not feel I had received such a call.

There were other concerns on my mind, and I had my personal doubt about everything in life and particularly, who I really was, and my earlier struggle with this issue was still very much on my mind. I can only describe the feeling as losing at times the sure knowledge of my deeper identity which I called My True Identity. It was a very strange feeling. My mind wandered and I thought of this earth as a very tiny mud and rock ball situated amid unlimited space and on which millions of humans moved around like insects.

I was one of the insects, and it made me feel very lost and lonely.

I realised that the root cause of my predicament was that I had stopped praying and reading the Bible or, for that matter, any book dealing with the human condition. I had cast myself loose and no longer had an anchor. Although, every week I would receive a letter from my father imploring me to read my Bible and to pray every day but such exhortations, far from touching me, merely caused me annoyance.

I was now a lost soul.

During this period, I met some interesting people, including a family in which everyone was a "totalitarian", that being they abstained from every kind of fermented drink and were vegetarians and followed the Unitarian faith. Although the two sons were very fit and rode huge distances on their bicycles, the family overall looked ill and "pasty faced". They offered me no indication of the route I should take in life. In fact, despite foregoing many things in life by abstinence, they did not seem to have anything to put in place instead.

They offered me no practical route.

There was no Baptist church in the small county town where I was living and so I attended a Congregational church. At first this church had no minister but after a while one was engaged; to my mind he was an imposing figure with his golden beard and looked very much like the pictures of Jesus Christ one sees hanging in some churches.

His first sermon was unforgettable. He lost touch with his congregation completely and I thought he had probably lost touch with God too. It was a painful experience for all concerned.

But on succeeding Sunday evenings this man, who had made such an unpromising start, preached a series of inspiring sermons which aroused support and strong interest in the town.

This minister was a working man, in addition to his clerical duties, and had a broad view of the world. He made me write a paper and read it to an audience; he also made me recite, he made me open debates, and he even persuaded me to sing. Maybe he saw me as a potential willing candidate to help him in his church duties... I am not sure how good my singing was, however, as when congratulated by a member of the audience, this person noted that I had interchanged the first and last verses. He added that I had sung the song "very well", at which my spirits rose, only to subside when he added, "Especially well, considering you did not know it". He then advised that it was a good plan to learn a song before singing it in public.

At the time of all this I was just eighteen years of age but looked more like sixteen. I thought the minister might have plans for me but fortunately he never asked me to preach in his place; this was a relief.

I was very sensitive about my ultra-youthful appearance, and everyone seemed to view me as a child whereas I wanted to be regarded as a man. However, there was nothing I could do about it other than to wait for the grey hairs and wrinkles to appear! They came in due course, but like many other things we long for when we are young, when they did arrive, I wondered why I had ever desired them.

Bicycling became my strong interest in those years, and it was very much a novelty. There was no suitable club in the area at the time, so we started one and it was supported enthusiastically, and the number of members grew quickly. I do not remember exactly how many we had but when we went for a Club ride we extended, two abreast, for what must have been several hundred yards.

On our first "run" out, the Club captain rode in front whilst the vice-captain rode behind us all to whip up stragglers; the captain himself wore a real bicycling suit consisting of a very tight pair of breeches, which were so tight at the knees that it made bending the knees difficult, and on his body he wore a tightly fitting tunic, rather like those worn by military bandsman, and with a lot of braid zig-zagging from side to side. On his head he wore a hard jockey cap with a large peak. I can only call it a monstrosity of a uniform which was clearly not designed by a cyclist.

Looking back on it today it must have been an extraordinary sight!

The rest of the riders would wear ordinary clothes and, after our first ride out as a Club, I do not recall the captain wearing the same egregiously constraining outfit again. I think once was enough for him.

Bicycles were a novelty in these days and not many people had ever seen one. Therefore, on completion of our first "run" out the captain led us though the town and it seemed as though every resident came out to join the throng, gazing at the spectacle of so many penny-farthing bicycles with their riders sitting aloft. They were to be rewarded again by a similar spectacle when we organised further bicycle race meetings to which riders from far and wide came. Perhaps the most memorable of all events we held was an illuminated bicycle parade with all the bicycles festooned with Chinese lanterns. This spectacle secured an applause!

Life in the small town was more interesting and agreeable than London. Outwardly everything seemed to be very good but, as in most societies, there were people one could so easily become involved with and be led astray to live a less than desirable life.

My life was akin to the pendulum of a clock; first I would swing to the right (good) and then to the left (the not so good).

During my first months in the town, I was positioned with the pendulum well out to the right but then I fell into the trap with a new group of friends by staying up late, playing cards and billiards into the small hours, and consuming far too many drinks.

I made many attempts to break away from the wild set of youngsters who had become my companions, but without success and decided that, once again, I had no option other than to break loose and make a fresh start elsewhere.

You may wonder about my spiritual development and aspirations for the future – I could see no clear road ahead.

The Way to know God is to trust him. If we do this, then we learn through experience and direct knowing that which is quite beyond the intellect.

His Wisdom Guiding

HT Hamblin

Chapter 7

More Wild Oats

It may be difficult for you, my reader, to understand how anyone, having had the spiritual experiences and the awakening I had when younger, could have fallen away so severely. I certainly had become "Henry the Wayward".

When I had my Awakening experiences, there was no one I could find at the time who could help me through the challenging process, and it was a case of the blind leading the blind. I had, earlier, been advised to get over it and be as other boys and forget the experiences. It is not surprising, therefore, that I fell into the proverbial ditch.

Having been cast adrift, as it were, I was destined to find out the hard way through experience which would incur suffering and distress on my part.

I have often wondered what might have happened had I been able to meet someone who knew about these things, such as what I have referred to as my Awakening, and of the ways of the Holy Spirit, for I am sure that it was something spiritual in my case. If I had such a person to talk to and who could help me understand what had happened to me then I might have become a fully awakened soul. But it was not to be then and would not happen until many years later.

If there is a lesson to be learnt from this experience it is surely that there should be more men and women of God available to help those in such situations as I found myself in. I have never met one but feel sure that there must be many other people who have had similar experiences to mine and who could have benefitted from help had it been available.

Anyway, with that as a prelude to this next chapter, it is time to move on with the story.

I left the small town in East Anglia with a certain amount of regret. The time there had been formative and generally enjoyable and, looking back at it now, it was a core part of my development.

I left Norwich on the first train in the morning and was destined for the area in the Midlands known as The Potteries. The journey took all day and involved changes of train, including a very long wait at Uttoxeter. Finally, very late in the evening I arrived at my destination for that day and found a room for the night in what was then called a "commercial hotel".

It was a strange experience in the hotel especially as everyone called each other "Sir". The other guests even addressed me as "Sir" which puzzled me as no one had ever called me by this pronoun before. But I was soon to realise that this was a formal mode of address between commercial travellers.

I did not sleep, as my bedroom overlooked a railway shunting yard which was busy all night!

But I still had more travelling to do and continued my journey west and duly arrived at my new place of employment the next day.

My new employer seemed taken aback by my youthful appearance and hesitated to allow me to start work. But as soon as I unpacked my tools, he was impressed by what he saw and raised no further objection. A good workman loves fine tools. He was clearly a good workman looking at the quality of things he had produced, and my tools were as fine a set as one could ever wish for.

So, with me, it was not a case of "my face is my fortune" but it was my kit of tools which was persuasive!

Socially, I found lodgings nearby, and, on being invited to enjoy hospitality with others, I informed everyone who invited me to drink with them that I was a teetotaller and hoped to remain so. I was tolerated.

I became interested in activities other than my work and bicycle-racing was one. I rode in races in nearby Port Vale and Crewe but without success. I found the air locally was not as fresh and bracing as that in East Anglia and never found that I could breathe as easily as normal. Perhaps it was that the air was polluted but, in that era, we were not conscious of such things. (Many years later I settled by the sea to benefit from the bracing air.)

However, there was one event that remains a clear memory and it was a week's bicycle tour of North Wales. My colleague for the trip was older than me but an experienced long-distance rider who would teach me much about the part of the country we were to visit.

By some miracle we chose the one good week of weather, August 1892 I recall, to begin our tour. Our penny-farthing bicycles were heavy and had solid tyres and were made heavier still when we loaded them up with photographic apparatus, a bellows camera, a tripod, and dozens of glass plates. I recall that each machine when loaded must have weighed in the order of seventy pounds.

The roads in those days were rough with a loose surface but despite these handicaps we achieved an impressive 110 miles on our first day.

We were not out to set records but to find beauty and photograph it. And we found beauty everywhere. I became speechless, possibly for the first time in my life. I have never been able to convey to anyone what my feelings were when I gazed at the Welsh mountains for the first time. (It would prove to be the only time in my life that I was in that part of the country.)

The many photographs my colleague took were technically very good but, to me when I saw them a few days after our trip, they were a disappointment. No photograph could, in my view, ever convey the majesty and inspiration of the sensation I had when gazing on those Welsh mountains.

The Welsh people were delightful and generous in their hospitality at every location we stopped at for the night. They charged us so little for a night's rest and food that I felt rather like a robber when I paid them the small amount they requested.

This holiday trip was, however, the one bright spot in a rather sombre picture. Although I had managed to keep on the "straight and narrow" for a while, I soon began to drift back into my old ways and began to socialise with people who enjoyed a drink or several. There must have been an atavistic strain in me which attracted me to them and vice versa. It was not my friends who were at fault but me in departing from the standard I had set for myself.

A very spiritual-minded friend of mine once wrote this to me: "All the evils generated in an interminable line of ghostly ancestors flow into the souls of men. These evils are modified by culture and external moralities, but the atavistic tendencies of every sin in the calendar are there just the same".

Whether or not this is true one can ponder, but if it is, I think it would be equally true to say that if we are potentially capable of committing the seven deadly sins, we are also potentially capable of going in the opposite direction to become aligned with God in the way taught by Jesus Christ. Remember the Biblical text: *"But to all who did receive Him, to those who believed in His name, He gave the right to become children of God"*. (John 1:12)

I have deduced that in this life we are positioned midway between Heaven and Hell. Metaphorically, if we look down, we attract thoughts and impulses of an infernal, sinful, nature. In contrast, if we extend our thoughts into a heavenly direction, we draw ourselves into a heavenly way of thinking and behaving.

The Lord's Prayer teaches us how to do this.

Alas, I was never taught this. I was totally ignorant of the power of thought or even of the fact that we could control our thoughts.

Indeed, those who were my spiritual guides and instructors in my early time with the church said that we could not help our thoughts. The implication of this was that we were powerless to do anything about our thoughts. It followed, therefore, that if sad thoughts came to an individual, that person would dwell on them to the detriment of their health and usefulness to society. Moreover, if depression crept upon them, they surrendered to it, thus becoming morbid and often pathological in their outlook. Sadly, such people would have had no idea that sad, negative thoughts could be ousted by the deliberate cultivation of joyous thoughts or that feelings of depression could be similarly defeated by applying the mind to the cultivation of pleasant thoughts.

I was taught that I could try to fight against evil thoughts, but I was not then aware that doing so could give the bad thoughts greater control over me. My experience has convinced me that fighting adverse thoughts, evil thoughts, merely serves to embed the ideas even more strongly in the mind.

On the other hand, supplanting the evil thoughts with positive ones is the best approach to solving this problem.

Suggestion is stronger than will-power and my experience is that it is always the victor over bad thoughts. Counter-suggestion, as the opposite of bad thinking, always wins.

Thus, my experience is that an evil thought is made stronger by fighting it whereas it can be defeated by cultivating a thought which is its opposite. Hatred can be overcome not by fighting it but by love. This was the message of Jesus.

The control of our thoughts is the all-important action but, as already mentioned, I knew nothing about this when I was in my final years living at home. After I had left home to become employed, I found myself wallowing in wrong thinking, not knowing that by doing so I was using the vast power of suggestion of my mind to my own detriment. I did not know it at the time, but I was letting loose powers of great potency, which in due course would sweep me off my feet and compel me to live the life which I had allowed my imagination to embrace.

My life became one of folly and wild behaviour.

But there was one woman, a neighbour, who declared that I could not be wholly bad because I was the only person who would nurse her baby when it was ill, the only one who could stop it crying, and the only one who would kiss it. I can even now remember that poor child as it cried all day long and was covered in sores, which was probably the cause of the distress. The baby cried when held by the mother but was content when I held it.

The baby eventually recovered fully.

Whether my ministering to it had anything to do with the recovery, I will never know. It may have been that my love and kisses imparted a healing touch but, if so, I was unaware of it.

In later years, when my mother suffered with arthritis in her hands, she always requested that I rub them and would not allow anyone else to do so. Thus, I often wondered whether I had a healing touch, although I was quite unconscious of having any such ability. In time my life would lead me not to be a healer of sick bodies but to be a healer of people's minds.

After I while I decided to have a complete change from the work I had been doing and moved to another town nearby where I found employment; it was another manifestation of my inability to persevere which had been, and was to remain, my problem for many years. However, instead of developing the work I was paid to do, at which I think I was pretty good, I decided to take on additional unpaid work on a farm. However, this experience revealed that, whilst I could create good work at a workbench, I was to prove a bad farm labourer.

The farmer himself was not a full-time farmer but a small tradesman undertaking farming to supplement his income. All it did for him, however, was to run him into further debt.

In addition, his paid labourer on the farm, a young boy, who had not received much in the way of an education did not enhance the farm's profitability and he and I were a central part of the problem. If the farmer had known anything about farming, he would not have entrusted his labourer and me to plough his field. You may think that I am exaggerating the story, but if anyone had watched us doing the ploughing, they would have burst out laughing. Let me elaborate.

To do the task we were given a heavy draught mare, and her partly broken colt. The mare was placid, but the colt was completely unbroken. At first the colt refused to move and then, without warning, dashed forward as though trying to win a race. And so, with the two beasts in harness with the plough behind them, we dashed forward with me in the front trying to control this strange team, while the boy behind tried in vain to plough a straight furrow. After a short burst the colt came to a halt, exhausted and with heaving flanks. And then when we had all recovered our breath, off dashed the colt again, but of course restrained by its mother. And so, we went up and down the field until at last our task was completed.

But never had there been such ploughing in that neighbourhood. Our furrows were all over the place and made us look like fools and the farm became a source of amusement to others living in the area.

The farmer was not at all pleased with our ragged handiwork, of course. However, we sowed the field with oats and raised a fair crop which was surprising as neither the boy nor I had ever done any ploughing before!

Although there was much agriculture in the area it was also an area of intensive mining. Collieries abounded and I had many friends amongst the colliers; I knew them well enough to be invited into their homes. They were a fine lot of men, very strong and hardworking, and good friends so long as you treated them decently. They were generous to a fault.

Therefore, when disaster came, as it sometimes did, it became a very sad business for everyone. I remember one disaster when a pit, which I knew quite well from visiting it, became flooded because the mining had accidentally broken into an old mine that was full of water. The result was great disaster, and some 120 homes were without their men and were desolate.

No one who has not lived among miners can understand what such a disaster means. The doors of the cottages would be left open day and night in case the good man returned. And the women, with shawls over their heads, kept watch at the pit head, waiting hour after hour, hoping, in vain, to hear some good news from the search parties.

And what men they were who made up the search parties! They risked their lives in failed attempts to rescue their imprisoned colleagues. Again and again, they were driven back and sometimes they had to be rescued themselves by others.

I have found it impossible to forget that anxious time. The days passed, and gradually all hope had to be abandoned; the cottage doors were closed at last – and the good men had not returned home.

My abiding memory is of the men in the search parties. They worked until they became so exhausted that they had to be sent home to rest and recuperate.

Some of them, who never seemed particularly daring in everyday life, proved themselves to be heroes in the hour of danger and disaster. I knew one of them quite well and would never have expected him to be a hero, but he was, and he was one of those later selected to go to London to be decorated by Queen Victoria.

They were a proud group of men and living amongst them had been inspirational.

I became mixed up with a much smaller disaster nearby. One morning we heard a rumbling sound, which we assumed must be an explosion underground, and so a group of us started running towards the pit head, fearing the worst. But as we approached, we ran past the colliery railway which went down the hill to join up with the main railway below and there we saw a dreadful picture of a locomotive turned upside down and resting on top of a coal wagon with its steam whistle sounding unceasingly. It dawned on us that there had been a locomotive boiler explosion. We ran to the site.

It was the grimmest scene I had ever witnessed. It was like a battlefield, according to an old soldier who was nearby. The locomotive had exploded and the dead and dying were all around us. I tried to help but became faint and sick and was only revived when a colleague made me take a drink from his flask of brandy. (Or it might have been whisky – I am not a good judge of these things.) This revived me and I was then able to assist the local nurse and others in the rescue party.

I was asked to accompany one of the seriously injured to hospital but having delivered the patient to the surgeon, he informed us that there was nothing he could do to save the man's life. About an hour later he came out of the operating theatre to tell us that our patient had died.

I found myself severely shaken by the experience and in the middle of the night I became delirious. It was my first experience of being with death and watching people die. Previously, with the mining disasters I had not witnessed death close-up but only bodies being retrieved from the pit.

These sad experiences were fundamental to the way I developed as a person.

Turning to more domestic issues, I was by now a friend of the local curate, who in turn had a friend living with him who used to preach in church and was due to be ordained soon. This young man had many serious conversations with me and attempted to interest me in the classical music he played on his piano, but I was not ready for this sort of music and could not appreciate; to me it was just meaningless noise.

And then he pressed me to follow his example and become a priest. He had all sorts of ideas about how one could develop to become more like Jesus. But this was not for me at the time, and I declined his proposals. He then moved away for a while.

Meanwhile, my health had deteriorated, and it was the same old story being repeated. I drifted into my old ways and began drinking, staying up late and generally demanding too much of my body.

My friend who was due to be ordained then re-appeared in my life and I shall never forget his sorrow at the state I had allowed myself to get into. He was earnest and felt sorry for me, but little did he know that I felt sorry for him, because, at the time, I was the one having all the conventional fun out of life, whilst he focused on his forthcoming ordination.

I was never to see him again, but I am sure he would have become one of the great "fishers of men", in the biblical sense.

Although the people around me expressed their kindness at my self-inflicted worsening condition I was not able to do anything about it. I would gladly have reformed but was unable to and it felt as though I was caught in a net from which escape was impossible. Alarmingly, I seemed to have no power to turn over a new leaf and make a fresh start.

It was at this juncture that I began to experience deep remorse. I would wake up in the morning, not merely with my usual hangover, but in a state of despair and desolation which was beyond description.

I was now locked in the depths of depression and despair.

I did not know it at the time, but I am now sure that this was the Holy Spirit dealing with me and pointing out that my life was on the wrong track. I needed to make a radical change.

Similar warnings came to me in later years, when outwardly I was most successful, with the barometer of life set fair for ever. But these warnings came to me more as a gentle nudge, before it was too late, to move me back to the correct road.

In all these experiences, I am sure God was at work on me.

Although I could secure as much work as I needed, I was all too often displaying my inherent laziness and lack of focus and, unsurprisingly, my work declined which was not surprising as I was interested in anything and everything which was outside my business. (Memories of trying to plough a field instead of working for my employer!)

And then I found that people I had long regarded as friends were turning against me; I concluded that I had outstayed my welcome in the town and that it was time to move on the fresh pastures.

I was longing for home.

By this time my father, I had learned, had started his own small business based on the South Coast, my parents having moved out of south London whilst I was away. This was the stimulus I needed and, as I felt jaded, the thought of living near the sea was very attractive. Also, I felt that if I could live at home with its strict rules and discipline, I might be able to overcome the irresponsible elements in my character and live a decent life again.

Little did I realise what lay in store for me; that I should meet my fate in the form of the lady who later became my wife. And little did I know then that I would be able to change my calling in life, and that without capital, I should start a successful business that is still functioning and well known, although I had moved away from it once it had become established. But that is a later story.

And so, I wound up my slender affairs, packed my tools and effects, what few there were, and retired quietly from the scene.

On the way home I visited an uncle of mine who had always been good to me and kept in contact by letter writing during my time away from home. He was a stabilising influence, and I shall always be grateful to him for his forbearance.

I arrived home by train and arrived at my parents' new home by the sea in Sussex just days before my 23rd birthday. My clothes were shabby and ill-fitting; there was little money in my pocket, and I had no idea what to do next. But I was home, and my rackety life was behind me.

But what of the future I wondered; always remembering the text from the Bible:

"...for whatsoever a man soweth that shall he also reap." (Galatians Ch 6:7-9)

There is no need to pray for anything, but only to commune with God, and to trust the Current which knows the way.

The Open Door

HT Hamblin

Part 2

Chapter 8

I Return Home

I had been away from home for a little over 5 years, but I felt 20 years older. I had sadness in my mind because I thought that all the best days of my life were behind me. On reflection, I must have been like an old man looking back over a long misspent life and ruminating on the past and I kept thinking of the "what might have been", which of course now could never be. I had adopted a negative view of my life having been through some wild and bitter experiences. It was entirely my doing and I never thought to blame anyone else.

Now safely back at home, I was taken to task by a friend I knew, who was a bit older than me, who told me in no uncertain terms that it was ridiculous for a young man like me to think and talk in this negative way. He advised me that I should acknowledge that I was still a young man with almost my whole life ahead of me, and that my future was rich with promise. I most certainly should not be looking at life like an old man with nothing but the grave ahead of him.

His reproach made an impact on me.

He went on to say that I needed to smarten up and that I would both look and feel a lot better if I wore decent well-fitting clothes. He thought I looked more like a scarecrow than a human being! I retorted that my clothes had been made by a good tailor and were not yet worn out. At which he laughed and responded that, as he was learning to be a tailor's cutter with a high-class firm, he knew quite a bit about clothes. And then he added: "I have never seen such badly-fitting clothes as yours". He had made his point!

As regards my expressed views about my misspent youth I told him that he just did not appreciate the turmoil I had been through. As far as I could tell, I had lived my life and made a mess of things. I felt that I had had my chance, the chance in life that comes to every man, and had wasted it and that nothing remained for me to look forward to.

In addition, I was worn out and run down from my frenetic pace of life, and from burning the candle at both ends, and now utter fatigue had hit me.

Anyway, I was near penniless and buying new clothes was beyond my means.

I knew I had to do something positive and felt that, if I could get a "blow" of real sea air, it could revive me. Therefore, using what little money I had left, I went out to sea, sometimes in small boats and at other times in larger pleasure paddle-steamers.

The sea worked its magic and I soon felt much better, to the extent that I started looking for work and in due course found employment, albeit with a most disagreeable man. The salary was modest and on a par with others in an era of low wages. However, my previously mentioned "genius for sarcasm" soon got me into trouble and out of work.

In those days, I had not learnt that a gentle answer can overturn wrath. Instead, I used to use sarcasm to such effect that the wrathful would get yet more angry. This behaviour did me no good at all and just seemed to create enemies wherever I went.

I did not bother to find other employment as a craftsman; I had quite enough work coming in from word-of-mouth recommendations anyway.

Several times during my life, and prior to having a stroke of good fortune, I have become aware of it before it happened. I remember one summer evening, after I had finished work, I went to the sea front and sat alone on a seat. I leant back, relaxed, and gazed over a calm sea when, quite suddenly, I became aware of a remarkable sense of peace and well-being. Quite suddenly, my usual fears and anxieties fell away, and I was conscious of being in a state of perfection. This beautiful feeling of peace and harmony lasted for several minutes before fading away.

The experience did indeed herald good fortune as it was not long after that I was to become engaged to the wonderful lady who, at the time of writing, 1947, has been my wife for over forty-four years. By any measurement, this was the best slice of good fortune which has ever come my way. Let me touch now on what she had let herself in for.

Through thick and thin, through storm and sunshine, through changing fortunes and through happiness and sorrow, my faithful partner for life has stood by me and never once faltered. It was not only a great adventure but a great act of faith on her part to entrust her life to a penniless youth, of uncertain temperament, without prospects, and with a record of failure.

But life with me was to prove even more trying for her than she could ever have envisaged.

Because, without warning or talking about it to anyone else, I decided to change my occupation completely and embark on a highly technical business as an optician, for which I was totally untrained but for which my earlier training at a workbench would be relevant.

Then, having built up this new business, and other similar ones which followed, until each was well-established, I decided then to make another big change in my forties and once again gave up the latest, and highly successful, optician business to live the life of a mystic and become a writer, of sorts. How my dear, patient wife tolerated all this I will never know, especially as such changes were a great strain on our resources.

I cannot remember how many times we moved house, first to the country and then into a town and back again. This must have been a huge challenge to her, but she never faltered or complained. I can never put into words adequately my tribute to her for her unfailing goodness, love, and faithfulness.

Many friends were sorry for the challenges my wife faced. One told her that she was afraid life would always be difficult because she was married to a mystic and that living with such people would always be a challenge.

But I am sure that, in their heart of hearts, they would not have had it otherwise. After all, what is the use of an easy life? Can it give satisfaction? The answer to both questions is surely no. The reason I say this so clearly is that I am certain that God's hand is in everything and that He has always been alongside us.

In the same way that I was alerted ahead of the event to the great fortune of meeting my wife-to-be, some twelve years later I had a similar experience of a sense of wellbeing just before I embarked on a great success in business. (I will come to this in a later chapter.)

But I am getting well ahead of myself and need to go back to the life immediately after my return home and being able to breathe in the refreshing sea air. It may seem strange that I managed to settle down so easily into a religious-minded home after my life with "the boys" in those five years away from home. In one environment, home, I was known for my pleasant demeanour and in the other, away from home, for my wild pranks and excesses. The reason I could settle back at home so readily was that I had become heartily sick of the life I had been leading and longed for stability and something different.

As the reader will, by now, have realised, my life in the early years had been one of extremes, first trying to be very good and then becoming very bad. It was as though I swung between following a God-given path to one that had much sin in it. From Light to Darkness and back again had been my mode of living. But now I was in the Light again and felt very comfortable in my new environment at home.

Of course, I had had to adjust my way of living; I had to guard my speech and avoid bad language and I needed to avoid temptation when passing a pub or a wine bar with the pleasant aromas they offered; I was ready for change and these attractions were soon forgotten.

Having been a smoker, my parents were both surprised and pleased that I was now an avid non-smoker, and they took the view that, if one neither smoked nor drank, then you were halfway to Heaven. But inwardly I knew this was not the case and that there was much more to it that just stopping doing some things.

I was welcomed to the Baptist church, where I discovered that my father had become a deacon and was playing an active part in running the services. However, as he led the congregation in prayer I would sit, barely listening, as my mind wandered to thinking of my past follies as well as wondering what the future might hold. I found the minister and his wife to be inspiring representatives of God and Heaven and they were universally respected. Although the minister moved on after a few years, he and I remained in contact until he died.

He had a direct bearing on the way my life would develop. When we first knew him, he was very orthodox and adhered to traditional doctrinal views and took the view that those people who did not share his views were wrong.

There was a gap of many years between the time he and his wife left our church and us meeting them again. When we eventually did meet again all those years later his outlook seemed to have changed. By this time the venture of *The Science of Thought* had become well established and he was most interested in it. I expected him to disapprove of my modern ideas and offer detailed criticism but was both surprised and pleased when he became enthusiastic and spoke of my work as a unique ministry towards which God had called me. He added that he prayed that I might be given strength and grace to bear the burden of it all and, moreover, he saw great things in store for *The Science of Thought*.

I feel sure that the influence of this good man, from the day we first met, came at the most opportune time in my life. Just when I had become tired of my juvenile life and my wild ride away from home, I had one of my amazing experiences. It was in 1896 and I described the event in *The Science of Thought Review* of September 1943, as follows:

"One night I felt that I must pray and knelt by the side of my bed. Immediately I became aware of the Divine Presence. I felt that God was near and that His presence filled the room. This Presence was real and tangible. It was warm and glowing; it was not merely a state of mind or consciousness. It was something more than that. It was as though the Lord Himself had come into the room and had come very close to me and that I had entered His aura, or whatever we may call the spiritual atmosphere which surrounds Him, and which is emitted from Him.

It is not possible to describe such an experience accurately. All care, anxiety and fear vanished, and I felt that I was cradled in Divine love, and poised in it and in the Eternal, effortlessly, just as the Heavenly bodies are poised, seemingly effortlessly, in space. The deep peace of the Eternal flowed through me like a river, yet at the same time it was as though I was being carried along on a stream of Divine bliss, and that the Lord and I were unified and became one in union for ever. There was I, cradled in God's inward peace, and floating out on to the bosom of an Infinite ocean of infinite bliss; yet, at the same time, His peace and His bliss flowed through me like a great river, and I was one with it, and paradoxically it seemed that I was the river itself.

But just as Peter and James and John were not allowed to remain on the mount of transfiguration, so it was with me. The night of blessed revealing came to an end; the blissful sense of the near Presence departed; the realisation of union was lost – and the vivid experience faded into a memory."

Living back at home with my parents, it was quite natural that I should be drawn in by the church to undertake evangelistic work, such as speaking at open air services, and at other churches and conducting services as well as preaching. But it was not my calling, and I did not excel or enjoy this type of work. As a rule, at such events, I felt very much alone with God far away; it made me rather miserable at times. Very occasionally I felt a sense of spiritual uplift, but I could not rely on any such inspiration as it was infrequent.

On these rare occasions of receiving a spiritual uplift, I became relaxed and at ease on the rostrum and did not feel alone but sensed a feeling of the spirit lifting me up. At this juncture, I found a stream of connected thoughts and ideas flowing into my mind and it was almost as though the thoughts came in and out came my words. It felt that what I was saying was being given to me without thought or effort on my part. Amazingly, when it was all over, I felt refreshed. And on these occasions, the audience would follow every word without even the slightest interruption. No one even coughed or cleared their throats.

But at other times, when I felt all alone, the opposite happened. My notes and preparation were inadequate, I could not achieve empathy with the audience and, clearly, they were not at all interested in what I was trying to say. This left both the audience and me exhausted. I am sure that the former would have been glad it was all over; I know I was.

I was concerned about this situation and asked myself: "Why on one occasion was speaking and preaching so satisfying to me and helpful to the people whereas at other times it was the opposite; unhelpful and exhausting?"

The only answer I could think of was that, on the relatively rare occasions it went well, I thought I must have been receiving help from a Spiritual presence which filled me with Spiritual qualities greater than my own. In this situation I concluded that it was not really me speaking but God through this Spiritual presence which came upon me. It was not a case of the Spirit guiding my tongue but rather that I was imparted with a stream of ideas and given the power to express them clearly so that everyone fully understood the message I was giving.

I pondered this. The conclusion I came to was that if I had freely welcomed it and depended on the Spirit being with me and working through me, then I could have become a true preacher from whom many would have been helped by what the Spirit prompted me to say. But I could not depend on the Spirit always being with me and it was only on rare occasions that this happened. From this I concluded that God or Spirit did not want me to become inspired this way.

I deduced that if a preacher was not able to be inspired, as I had been on a few occasions, then it would be best for all concerned that he gave up preaching. If God was not present, then the message would not be meaningful.

Another conclusion I came to was that I had never felt a call to preach and that, without such a call, I had no right to even think of becoming one. This proved to be a sound judgement.

Little did I think then of what God had in store for me.

I felt increasingly sure that the work I was doing with the church was too much in the old "rut of circumstance" and a continuation of my earlier life with it. I was sure that I needed to spread my wings and rise out of the current pattern of life.

I felt that life should be an adventure instead of a continuing round of monotony. But, I wondered, how could I find an opening? Deep down I knew that I did not wish to remain held back in life, below those who, by virtue of their higher social standing, were able to live a quite different life from ours. I was tired of living a life that was little different to being in a herd of farm animals where the whip of circumstance controlled one's life. I felt that it was time I had a turn at "cracking the whip" by being the master rather than the employed.

This clearly shows that my motives, at the time, were selfish and that, because of this, I would eventually suffer. However, God gives us plenty of rope to enable us to learn from experience.

This He did in my case, as subsequent chapters will reveal.

'The glorious riches of this mystery, which is Christ in you, the hope of glory' (Colossians 1.27)

Difficulties and drawbacks are only to test our metal, and all who believe they can succeed, and will trust in the Power within them, will succeed, and there is nothing on earth that can stop their progress .

The Fundamentals of True Success

HT Hamblin

Chapter 9

Important Moves

This story of my life may seem very material, but most of my time was spent in dealing with practical things and earning just enough to keep the wolf from the door. I was, however, not content with that and had a clear notion that I needed to develop my life so that I was never troubled by the wolf again.

I was not satisfied with what I was doing in life as there seemed to be no future; the work I was undertaking was in a declining industry. What I needed to find was work which I could build on and grow. This feeling was not just because I wanted to progress in life but because I found myself driven by a pioneering spirit, although, at the time, I did not realise I had this quality.

After some experience in business, I discovered that what I enjoyed, and was best at, was building up a new one from nothing. But then I found that, once the business had become established and profitable, I lost interest in it and started looking at other potential enterprises and would dispose of what I had created for a meagre return, thereby enabling others to benefit from the business idea which I had created.

I went on to repeat this process for much of my early working life, allowing others to reap fortunes from businesses which I had created and nurtured only then to pass them on. And I have been quite content to do this as I have little affection for the routine of a daily task. I was no "come day, go day, God send Sunday" as they used to say when I was a child. I just loved the fight and struggle against the odds of creating something new. That was the challenge which motivated me.

My parents would probably have said that this pattern of behaviour was due to my weakness of character together with my lack of staying power, and my inability to finish anything I started. My mother would probably have quoted her favourite text to me once again: "Unstable as water, thou shalt not excel".

Perhaps that may have been one of the reasons for my behaviour and at the time I thought this to be the sole cause of my frequent changes. But now that I can look back on my life, I can see that it was my pioneering spirit which was the main motivator.

Consequently, I had a determination to launch a new enterprise and create something new which would grow rather than hang on to a decaying business which would shrink over the years and become more and more impoverished. The only thing driving me was to create something new. Nothing else would satisfy me.

With this determination I clearly had to move on to a new path. As usual, everything seemed to be against me. I had no money, and worse than that, I was in debt and not even solvent.

In addition, I was engaged to be married but could not afford to marry, so my fiancée and I could not move forward. Moreover, I had received no training for the new venture I had in mind and yet I would be voluntarily leaving an area of work for which I was well qualified, but which yielded me very little in financial terms.

Nothing could have looked more hopeless to an outsider than this new wild, madcap, and foolish idea of mine. But on the inside, I was driven by my pioneering spirit which braves all and dares all.

My life had taught me that it is best to be daring and to move forward all the time rather than hold back and stay in one's own comfort zone for safety. When I have held back in an enterprise and played for safety, I have invariably suffered loss and had difficulty.

I have found that, if we hold back, everything slips from us. My life has taught me clearly that we must always move forward whilst trying to identify and stay aligned with the Divine pattern for one's life, as it unfolds.

The Divine pattern was unfolding in my life although, at the time, I did not know it. Rather the opposite, as the hardships of my life did not seem at all Divine to me.

However, there was only one thing to be done and that was to move forward. In doing so, I had to accept that I was not industrious by nature, unlike some of my friends who possessed huge powers of application and energy. Alas, I could not join their ranks and just had to admire them from a distance. But I knew I had to move forward myself. There was no other option open to me that I could see.

I had learnt that, if I was truly focused on achieving a goal, I could work as hard as anyone to reach it. Despite my earlier relatively poor performance in my trade at a workbench and my "stops and starts", I knew deep down that I had the ability to achieve greater things. I had found that difficulties and initial failure acted to spur me on and make me even more determined to achieve my goals.

Moreover, I had, unknowingly at the time, learnt that imagination can be stronger than the will. In my case, I had discovered that using my imagination to visualise achieving my goal more than compensated for my weakness of will and inherent laziness. Using this approach, I saw the task I had envisaged as being accomplished and this was a powerful spur to my efforts.

If we use our imagination to good effect, we will soon see progress towards the envisaged objective. It is a very powerful tool to use.

However, as my new objective was to enter the optician trade, I needed to have some relevant training and then pass an examination so that I could be awarded the appropriate diploma. This was going to ask a lot of me as I had, as a rule, tended to fail examinations. Annoyingly, I had found that examiners had a disconcerting habit of asking questions about which I knew nothing. But it had to be done and the only issue was how it was to be done.

It was a challenge, as I already needed to work long hours at my workbench just to earn enough to live. I could not afford tuition or to hire a coach, so the only thing to do was to teach myself.

What I did was to do my normal task at my workbench until about 10pm and then, once other people had gone to bed, I would get out my books and learn all that they had to teach me. Also, I made simple experiments to satisfy myself that I could see objectively that the text-book theory worked. It was not easy, of course, mainly due to my lack of education. How much I regretted having wasted my opportunities at school!

But still, I made progress, and must have absorbed useful knowledge because, when subsequently I went to London to sit my examination, to my surprise and delight, I passed. It was an even greater surprise to my parents.

Thus, I secured a foot on the first rung of a ladder to a potential career as an optician. It was a very humble beginning. I was aged 25.

My next task was to exploit this new opportunity. The first challenge was to find suitable premises in our town of Littlehampton on the South Coast of England and then equip it. But how was I to do this as I had no money? I knew exactly what I needed but had no idea about how to go about it.

"One step at a time" has always been my motto. Thus, as soon as I found the premises I wanted in a reasonably affluent part of town, I plucked up my courage and went to see the landlord. He was a pleasant man but very curious about me. He wanted to know too much, I thought. He asked all about me, my parents, and the detail about the business I intended to establish. Perfectly reasonable questions for a landlord to ask of a prospective tenant but, for me, an experience well beyond what I was used to. How did I know I could pay the rent? In fact, he bombarded me and probed me with every possible question, and I took care to answer him fully.

Then he asked for references, and I had to admit that I had none. But I showed him my diploma and the challenge I faced in securing it and this seemed to please him.

The upshot of the interview was that I came away with the key to the premises in my pocket.

That was the first step achieved, but now I needed to have it fitted out. Not quite knowing how to go about this, I found a friend I knew, who was a builder, and told him of my aspiration and stressed that I was completely without capital or financial reserves. To my delight, he must-have believed in me, because he agreed to do everything I wanted but with payment later.

Next, I went to London to meet with the principal of a specialist optical supplier from whom I would need display and testing equipment as well as stock for my proposed new ophthalmic business. I explained to them that I had no money and that they might have to wait a long time for payment. After many questions, they too agreed. Thus, there was now a clear path ahead for this new venture.

I was thus committed to starting a completely new life as an optician.

Once the shop had been fully fitted out, the great day arrived when we opened for the first time. But there would be a rocky road ahead.

The initial monetary returns were unsatisfactory. Although I could take a small income, there was insufficient surplus to pay off the builder and the wholesaler. Thus, I was faced with a long struggle and there was no clear end in sight. The builder seemed almost to live on my doorstep, seeking a cheque from me for all his work. And on top of that there was rent owing and rates to pay, and more. But worst of all was the demand from my London supplier for payment!

The situation could have been tragic but for my pioneering spirit. Strangely, the more difficult things became, the more I enjoyed life.

I eased the problem of my debt with the wholesaler by providing Bills of Acceptance payable in three months. This provided some breathing space but merely deferred the payment deadline as at the end of the three months I would have to make payment or my credit would have been ruined and, of course, I was depending entirely on credit. In the event, I was able to settle all these debts by the due dates.

But there was one occasion when it was "touch and go". It was the final day of an Acceptance period and I needed to pay the money in to my bank before the end of the working day. The deadline was approaching, and I remember running as fast as I could to the bank, arriving just before closing time, I literally slammed the money on to the counter and gasped: "Here's the money, pay that bill please". But, they responded, "We have sent the Acceptance back as unpaid. There was no money in your account to meet it, so we sent it back".

I responded: "What do you mean, 'sent it back'?" I added with an aggrieved tone: "The money is here; today is the due date, and my instructions to you are to pay that bill and on no account pass the matter back to my supplier as unpaid". But still the bank staff protested.

Hearing the altercation, the Manager came out of his inner sanctum and wanted to know what the problem was. "Problem?" I said, "Yes, indeed we do have one, a big one". Then I told him the whole story but even he came up with the same words his staff had used: "But we have sent the Acceptance back, you gave us no instructions and there was not enough money in your account, so we sent it back". "Look here," I said, "Today is the date the amount is due, and, on this date, I have paid in enough to meet it and my instructions to you are to pay it, and on no account to send the Acceptance back as unpaid". I added: "For you it is just a matter of convenience, but for me it is a matter of life and death for my business".

The Manager capitulated and promised to retrieve the Acceptance and pay it. So that was that!

Those were exciting times. But later, when everything was paid off, and there were no bills to meet, I found life much less exciting.

So that is the end of the story about how I started a business without a single penny of capital. Of course, things have changed today but such hazardous adventures were the spice of life to me, and I repeated the same sort of business creation several times, with each one on a larger scale... until I left business forever. But you will have to read on to follow that phase of my life.

Meanwhile, I think it will be helpful to examine in more detail my experience of forming a business. When I did this, I was, as already mentioned, only twenty-five years of age, although I was often told that I looked closer to age nineteen. One result of this over-young look was that many potential customers would not come to me because they thought I lacked experience. I had to do something drastic to correct my young looks and, as I could not turn my hair grey or create age-creases in my face, I did the only thing possible, and that was to grow a beard.

In those days, beards among the mature and middle aged were common, but for a youngster in his twenties to grow one was considered distinctly unusual. However, I persisted, although the first few months were challenging both for me and my relatives. Initially, the beard did not grow in the way I wanted but patience was a virtue and in time I looked years older, which was what I wanted.

As I write this in 1946, at the age of seventy-three, I look my age and yet some people suggest I might want to shave it all off. But I normally retort: "Why would I want to look sixty-three instead of my real age, and what good would it do?"

In business I found that looking older was a benefit, as it implied wisdom and experience. It also made me look peculiar in the minds of some observers, although I found this was also advantageous. I realised that if a young man wants to progress in business or a profession it can be helpful to look different from others. Thus, my advice to a young person is to stand out from the great mass of other people; you may not be a genius but looking different can draw attention, which is part-way to success.

I mentioned earlier the power which can come to you from imagination. This should have applied to me at the age I was at but, in my mind, I had not yet worked out how to use the power of thought. Instead, I would go about life in the usual way and probably hindered myself by wrong thinking; worrying about how to save a penny here or there when it could have been more productive to focus on the bigger picture rather than the minutiae of daily life.

Now I know that, had I envisaged a larger and fuller life and prosperity for the business, I could have become more successful and been spared much worry.

My experience revealed that many of our troubles and limitations can be triggered by inappropriate use of our power of imagination. The German philosopher Jakob Böhme (1575 -1624), who was a Christian mystic and Lutheran Protestant theologian, called it the use of the "false imagination". I would prefer to describe it as the misuse of the imagination, because this power can be used rightly or wrongly, either constructively or destructively.

In my case, in this first business I started, I did not help myself and focused on my limitations rather than my strengths. I was forever trying to adjust matters by thinking of cheese-paring economies and was using my imagination to my own detriment. In my mind I was unknowingly focusing on the lack of money and the limitations of the business so that they became the centre of my attention. What I should have done was focus on the Truth about life as envisaged by God, which is a state of perfection and completeness, the very opposite of my concern about the limitations I faced and life's imperfections. I am sure that if I had held the Divine idea of perfection and completeness in my mind, instead of worrying about saving pennies, it would have made a huge difference.

If I had adopted this enlightened approach, I would not have had to run to the bank at the very last minute, and arrive in a state of exhaustion, to pay a bill with money I had just managed to borrow from a friend...

This sort of thing was exciting, and no doubt better than being in breach of the payment rules. However, it was not good business practice and, in time, it had a destructive effect on my health, as the next chapter will show.

Above all, although my life was still exciting, I was acutely aware that I was engaged to be married and yet was miserably off financially and there seemed little prospect of getting married. My wife-to-be was patient, most patient, and how she endured it is beyond my comprehension. Alas, what she endured then was as nothing compared to what she would have to endure after we were married. But that is another story.

I only wish that in those days I had known what I later knew! But I expect most of us can say that.

However, despite this rather negative discourse, I must have made use of my imagination to some extent, although without realising it, for how else could I have started a business with absolutely no money? Unwittingly, I had the imagination to do so from which success was eventually won.

But mindful of my religious background, I need to explain the role of prayer in my enterprise. I regret to say that I cannot remember making much use of prayer and was focused almost entirely on the day-to-day needs of the business; I was operating alone.

My neglect of prayer was probably because I had been brought up to regard prayer as either asking God to do things or not to do them. We prayed by asking God to do just what we wanted Him to do or to give us what we wanted. My experience is that this kind of prayer is of little use. For example, I used to pray earnestly for a desired outcome but the more I prayed the worse the situation became. If I gave up praying things would get better.

I did not know then that the type of prayer I had been using can be counterproductive and can push the goodness of life away from us rather than bring it closer. I did not know then that in prayer we should keep our mind focused on God. At that time, I had not discovered that keeping this focus brings the perfect peace of God to us, but also the joy of life which comes with the Divine love emanating from God.

I had then no idea of such a thing as opening my mind to what I call Divine adjustment, Infinite wisdom, and Infinite love. Indeed, despite my fairly long experience of denominational religion, I had never even heard of such ideas.

There was still a difficult road ahead for my life before I learnt to live in Harmony and Peace in the way God had intended.

The way of the Spirit is Harmony and Peace.

HT Hamblin

Chapter 10

Through the Dark Valley

The doctor looked serious and stood looking at his thermometer. I did not like the situation at all either. I said: "I'm quite sure there is nothing much the matter. I have felt like this before, and your predecessor gave me something for my liver and in a day or two I was all right again". Somehow, what I said did not sound convincing, least of all to me. The doctor continued to look grave, and I pressed him again to give me a dose of medicine for my liver.

He relented and he gave me my requested "dose" and allowed me to go back to work for a day or two, but he continued to look grave.

When I departed, he must have wondered who the doctor was, he or me, for as usual I had my own way, only in my case it was to prove the wrong way.

The two days passed but I was still feeling ill, a bit worse, in fact, and went to see him again, and had to admit that I was no better. Again, out came the thermometer followed by the same grave look of two days ago. He commented: "So your diagnosis was not correct after all?" He then became firm with me and told me to go to bed and stay there until he came to see me and on no account to eat anything. He added that he suspected I had contracted typhoid fever which he later confirmed.

So, I called a few friends, bidding them good-bye for a season as I expected to be in bed for six weeks at least. Then it was home to bed.

I was far from alone in my predicament and knew of others with the same illness, which was common in those days.

And so, I sank into what I call the Dark Valley. Every day I became weaker and thinner. I was lying there with a bag of ice on my head and eau-de-cologne cloths on my forehead and I sank steadily lower, down to the very lowest ebb when it did not seem possible to continue. I remember that during these days our new minister came and knelt at my bedside and spoke in very subdued tones, giving words of encouragement and hope.

Then came the crisis, the corner which had to be turned, and which by the grace of God was turned and in due course, the return of a normal temperature followed by a slow convalescence.

During the whole of this long illness, I was nursed by my mother, as we could not afford to employ a trained nurse. My mother, however, was used to nursing people through long illnesses as she had done for several relatives and friends over the years. By the time of my incarceration, she was aged sixty and becoming worn out from all her travails, which included helping in my father's business. I am sure that nursing me through my long illness would have been a severe strain for her, but she displayed wonderful love and commitment to me throughout those long weeks. I sometimes wonder whether children fully appreciate what their parents do for them.

The time came when I was allowed to go for a walk. I was a walking skeleton, so I was told, but improved rapidly, although not to anywhere near as well as I was before the illness. And then my recovery stalled, and it was decided that my mother and I should go away for a time so that both of us could recuperate together. This was made possible by the generosity of friends who were almost as poor as we were.

The business, meanwhile, had been in the good hands of my brother, who had fortunately joined as a partner not long before my illness.

It was quite clear that my mother and I both needed a long rest and so we set off to the bracing climate on the coast of East Anglia, a part of England for which I shall always cherish a deep affection. I was glad to be back there after 10 years away. My mother and I stayed some months together living in Lowestoft before she went home, leaving me to fend for myself.

That part of Suffolk was lovely in the summer, enabling one to travel to swim in the Norfolk Broads or take a boat out for the day, but in the winter, gales and floods became the norm and it was exciting, and not a little traumatic, to be an onlooker of shipwrecks from the safety of the sea front at Lowestoft, and of rescues by breeches-buoy and lifeboat.

Once again, I began to feel the life blood returning and I found myself starting to envisage creating a new business.

At about the time my mother went home I found myself involved with the local Baptist church and this involvement grew substantially whilst I was there. The minister was only a few years older than I was and he and I became friends, together with another particular friend of his who was the local YMCA (Young Men's Christian Association) secretary. It was a revelation to sit at supper with them both and listen to their conversation. They were both extremely well educated, and, in conversation, their quips, jests and banter were so clever that I sat enthralled by them. This was a new experience and cultural education for me.

From that day I tried to speak more correctly and in a less uncultured manner. This friendship was a preparation for a time in the future when I would be meeting those who were far above me in the social order of those days, without feeling at a disadvantage because of my lowly birth and education. Other people I met were very friendly as well and invited me to their homes and into their hearts.

On Sundays my YMCA secretary friend sent me anywhere and everywhere to speak or to preach; he even made me sing! I am not sure that my audiences enjoyed my singing or preaching, but they displayed wonderful powers of endurance. Some even looked pleased, or maybe relieved, when they were quite sure it was all over and that I had finished.

One Saturday evening the assistant Congregational minister called me and he was clearly in some difficulty. His chief had been taken ill suddenly and he, the assistant minister, would have to take his place. This would make it impossible for him to take the service at their branch church a few miles away, so would I be able to take his place, he asked?

I protested, pointing out that I would have little time to prepare. But he was persistent and clearly very concerned about the situation; reluctantly, I consented, but on the condition that the YMCA secretary accompanied me to give moral support. The secretary agreed.

Thus, the next morning we set off to the church. I was completely unprepared due to lack of time and felt entirely lost and devoid of inspiration. But I should not have been so anxious, as God had called me to this experience and He would see me through it. But my mind was in a whirl and refused to become composed.

Looking back now, I think I was suffering only from stage fright!

At the sight of our destination, I found that, instead of little hall with country folk as the congregation, it was a substantial and clearly flourishing suburban church with a large congregation. I was perturbed and would have preferred to have turned round and returned the way I had come. But the secretary led me on and into the building.

There we were greeted, and I was asked by an official: "Have I the pleasure of speaking to this morning's preacher?" Feeling a bit like an accused in a court being asked how he wished to plead, guilty or not guilty, I signified that indeed I was. Whereupon we were led to the vestry to be briefed on the order of service and, somewhat alarmingly, I was informed that there was a Churching to be included in the service for a mother who had just had a baby. "Churching?" I gasped, not knowing anything about such a ceremony. I asked the church official if there was anything in a prayer book as a guide, but he said there was not and that their usual minister made it up as he went along. He advised me that it would be appropriate to offer up a simple prayer of thanks to God for the new life given. There was no time for more preparation as it was by then eleven o'clock and the scheduled time for the service to begin.

On entering the church, I was alarmed to see the size of the congregation, and by the look of them all, they seemed far too intelligent and well educated and likely to be a challenging audience to deliver my sermon to. They looked as though they were expecting something special, but there I was sitting in misery, with no sermon planned, and not even a biblical text to use as the basis of that sermon. I was in despair.

I turned over the leaves of the New Testament I had with me and, quite by chance, opened it at the second chapter of the first epistle of John, verses 15 to 17:

"*Do not love the world or anything in the world. If anyone loves the world, love for the Father is not in them. For everything in the world—the lust of the flesh, the lust of the eyes, and the pride of life—comes not from the Father but from the world. The world and its desires pass away, but whoever does the will of God lives forever*". (1 John 2:15-17)

At once this gave me the inspiration I so desperately needed, and I felt the burden I was under lifted from me. Quite suddenly I was filled with joy and peace and the feeling of the Presence, which I had first experienced at my baptism, was with me again, I felt inspired.

The service progressed and I no longer felt any fear or dread and even the thought of the Churching ceremony no longer concerned me.

I now had my text which was the inspiration I needed for my sermon, although I did not immediately know what I was going to say. But I was now confident that God had given me the right text and that He would guide me in the delivery of my sermon.

And this was my inspiration, because, when I read out the words of scripture, I found myself entering into what I can only describe as a larger consciousness, and saw, as though in a vision I can only describe as: "all life and humanity spread out before me. I saw men lusting and striving, grasping, and scrambling, clutching eagerly at the baubles of life, and failing to hold them, then being caught in eddies which drew them down and out of sight".

For a short time, I seemed to be in another dimension having what I can only describe as Cosmic Vision. I felt as though I was on a mountain top, looking down at a sea of faces and with an intense pity in my heart. I remembered another Biblical text:

"For what shall it profit a man, if he shall gain the whole world, but lose his soul?" (Mark 8:36).

As I stood there I felt as though I was able to see into the hearts of struggling men and women. This gave me the basis of my sermon.

I could see the message I wished to impart all so clearly and received the impression that the congregation could also. Truly I felt the Presence that had visited me before, and it felt to me as we were all in harmony with our thoughts. To me it felt as if we were all caught up in a state of insight into the Cosmic, spiritual, realm and, once again, I felt that the Holy Spirit was with me.

I concluded my sermon with the positive note of: *"The world and its desires pass away, but whoever does the will of God lives forever".* (1 John 2:17)

Yes, I stressed, that is all it requires; do the will of God. This acceptance does not require us to believe in any doctrine which might affront our intelligence, or sense of justice, but just do the will of God. If we do so, we abide forever, for the will of God is the Divine Order which never changes or ages.

When I felt that I had said everything that the Presence was inspiring me to say, I closed my sermon and shortly after the service ended.

Thus ended one of the greatest experiences of my life.

Unsurprisingly, I was asked several times if I would go to the same church again as the congregation was asking for me. But each time I refused. I knew that I had given an inspired deliverance in special circumstances, and I knew also that I could not expect it to happen again. I felt, deep down, that I was not called to be a preacher and that if I were to go there again, the result could be very different.

However, the minister asked me later to be the speaker at a special meeting he was planning to hold to deliberate on prayer. The special meeting was to be held in the church on a week-day evening. Why he chose me to be the sole speaker I never discovered, especially as I was never one to go to Prayer Meetings, let alone to be prominent at one. However, the minister had probably assessed, correctly, that I felt that private prayer and personal devotions were more important than public prayer. By then I had realised that the inner life of an individual was dependent on private prayer.

The minister took the chair at the meeting and introduced me. The audience was large, and I noticed that the church secretary, who was the same YMCA secretary who had brought me on my first visit, was amongst them. I knew him to be a real man of prayer and I thought that he should have been giving the address as he was far more experienced than I was as a mere tyro. But, having been asked to speak I clearly had to do so as I had promised.

First the minister gave his views, which were just the ordinary ideas of prayer, such as praying for things, and telling God what to do. He took some time over this and then called me to speak.

In doing so I had been given liberty to say as I wished but not to criticise what the minister had said.

I stood up and, in effect, short circuited what he had just said by saying that real prayer was finding God and realising His Presence which is there available to everyone who seeks it. Also, I said that asking for things was not necessary, and that the only thing necessary was to move close to God, or "know" God as it is sometimes described. Praying that God's will be done is a much better approach than making specific requests.

As I was giving my address, I glanced at the church secretary and noted that he was almost jumping out of his seat with excitement. He clearly knew what I was speaking about even if the minister did not.

In those days, I was only a beginner, and my ideas were not then fully formed. However, I felt sure that the way I had been led by the Spirit was showing me the way God was guiding me. He was not leading me through the intellect, or through doctrines or theories, but through experience. I did not attempt to put any labels on what had happened or came to me. I simply knew that a Presence came to me and that at times I had been caught up in God.

By contrast, my upbringing and early church involvement had involved a very strict doctrine. It had been rammed into me, and reiterated again and again, that I must believe in a particular doctrine because it was the only right one, and all who did not believe and accept it were doomed to eternal punishment. I found this strange as I had also been taught that God was a God of love, mercy, and compassion,

Whenever I pointed out, in my early years, that Jesus did not teach a particular doctrine at all and that what He did teach did not seem to be being lived up to by those who accepted the doctrine, I was rigorously put down. I was led to believe that the Sermon on the Mount was merely there for us to read but not to follow.

Not being good at argument, and being the youngest in the family,

I generally got crushed. However, I felt that I had a strong case and was also pretty sure that my parents and teachers were simply deluded. They were fixed in their views and afraid to question them, or to reason, or think for themselves, for fear of being condemned to everlasting punishment.

It became clear to me that the only thing I could really *know* about God was what I discovered from experience. Also, I was equally sure that I could find God by Him revealing Himself to me through my personal experience.

I realised that He was doing this but, owing to my sinfulness, frailty, and the Dark Forces which assailed me, my progress continued to be slow and painful.

It would become even more painful as subsequent chapters will reveal but, looking back, I would not have had it otherwise.

Meanwhile, shortly after I was back at work after my illness and recuperation, we secured much better premises in the very best part of Littlehampton, on a long lease and with favourable terms. This seemed to be the opportune moment to hand over the business fully to my brother.

It was time for me to move on.

Praying for things ... is all right for beginners ... one enters the true Path only when one has passed from this stage to the next one, wherein we realise that there is no need to pray for anything, but only to commune with God, and to trust the Current which knows the way.

The Open Door
HT Hamblin

Chapter 11

Again I Launch Out

Whilst much had been happening to me on the East Coast, my wife-to-be was living on the South Coast. This was an unsatisfactory situation and, although I was still a "bird of passage", not knowing where I would be going to next, we decided to get married. As we had been engaged for five years we could not be accused of "marrying in haste".

So, everything was arranged, and the day before the wedding I travelled down to the South Coast. We had a quiet wedding, for that was what we both wanted, and the next day my wife and I travelled westwards to the borders of Hampshire and Sussex. After a few days there we went to my beloved East Anglia again, where we were received generously by the many friends I had made previously. Interestingly, they used an expression I had not come across before by saying to my wife: "I am wholly pleased to meet you".

At first, we lived in Lowestoft but, as summer approached, we moved two miles into the country and shared a small house with a delightful couple, a farm labourer and his wife, with whom we became friends for life and were separated only by their later passings.

Being in the country was perfect for us both and to this day I can recall the woods opposite our bedroom window with the wood pigeons seemingly calling me to breakfast each morning, for their cooing sounded like "Your breakfast is ready, your breakfast is ready, your..." and then they would break off short and refuse to complete the sentence.

Despite my wife and I being on holiday it proved impossible to resist a request from a local businessman friend to help organise a big church fund-raising event. One of my tasks was to produce a substantial brochure. Naturally, the church minister wrote a foreword for it but when I read it, I found it rather bland and unlikely to attract people. And so, without reference to other members of the organising team, I wrote my own version on more humorous lines. I felt I knew what would draw people to the event and let myself go in my writing. It worked and we had a great success. But I always felt guilty about discarding the minister's message for my own and feel sorry now that I acted in such a high-handed way.

On our holiday, and on fine summer days, we would hire a four-oared skiff and go for a long row on the Norfolk Broads. In those days we had plenty of privacy as there were hardly any craft on the water. Also, we much enjoyed country walks and rambles by the sea.

We had both always been interested in flowers and naturally we became involved in the local Flower Show. Although we had nothing to show ourselves, we helped our many friends and were as pleased and excited as they were when they had successes. This show was to be a harbinger of my wife's later passionate interest in horticulture in general and especially flowers. And my first publication when I became a writer was *The Message of a Flower*.

This idyllic existence could not go on forever and life was already beckoning us to go elsewhere and leave the bracing sea air and bright sunshine. We were to go to the smoke and gloom of the London metropolis.

It seemed a pity that this had to be and, if we had been able to make our home in East Anglia, as our friends had done, I am sure we could have been happy. But the call of enterprise was too strong for me to ignore and so London it had to be.

But why was it we could not stay? Why was it that life beckoned us to a huge city with all its smoke and gloom?

The answer is twofold. First, I was experiencing again some of the urges I had when younger to lift myself out of the austerities of being in the "lower middle class" of society. I vowed to myself that I would change all that and, somehow, climb to the top. And second, I felt that the pattern of my life, known only to God, was working itself out through me and that I had no option other than to follow the instinct. Whatever the cause might be, life was beckoning me to other spheres and to more adventures in the world of business.

Therefore, we said goodbye to our friends and left East Anglia as our home forever, only to return occasionally for holidays. We left with feelings of regret but, when life calls, we must always obey; the call of life cannot be avoided. One must obey or perish.

And thus, we moved on and I was reminded of Genesis 12:1 where Abraham obeyed the call of God: *"Go from your country, your people and your father's household to the land I will show you."* Our own venture was to be a most precarious one and the future was most uncertain.

But life was beckoning us, and I wondered if it was God calling?

Things were not easy, either for my wife or me. My family were against my plan to set up another enterprise and discouraged what they saw as an ill-conceived venture. But I was sure that I had to embark on it. I had already left the partnership business at Littlehampton to my brother, giving him the whole of it. As was to become my habit, I had started it without any capital.

Once this was done, I felt free to devote myself wholeheartedly to my new venture, to establish ophthalmic businesses in London.

On looking back, I recall that every move I have ever made in life, from the very first effort to get out of the rut to the present time, has been opposed by my relatives, friends, and would-be advisers. To them, nothing I proposed to do was ever right. I could never even propose to make a change, or do anything new, without a huge amount of argument with those who tried to throw a wet blanket over every idea I put forward. Consequently, everything I achieved was done in the face of apparent stone-walled opposition.

I mention this to encourage others who may have been born in difficult circumstances. If you are in that situation and wish to lift yourself out of poverty or poor conditions, then you must go ahead despite opposition. If you listen to those who are in a rut themselves, without a plan to progress out of it, then you yourself will never escape from it. However, if going into a partnership with another person, make sure you find someone with a positive attitude of mind, with a streak of enterprise and daring, rather than of a play-for-safety person.

Of course, not everyone can be a high achiever, but if we are born into poverty that should not inhibit a person's ambition. Instead, such a person should strike out and follow his or her ambition. The Divine forces will be there to help, but the individual must take the initial step.

My new venture certainly required a level of faith, as the first premises we had committed to were dilapidated and almost derelict. They had been unoccupied for many years, and nobody wanted them as they were poorly situated and looked unattractive. Other people thought we were fools for taking the lease, but we did so on as long a term as possible. I say "we" as it was now my wife and I who would function as the business.

Our critics did not know what our plans were, and they certainly did not know what was going on in my head. But they would soon see, as it was not long before we were ready for business with a promising level of trade from the beginning although it required a lot of work and late hours. Whilst some people like just to pass the time of day, I was busy from the beginning of this new venture, and it was a case of trying to keep pace with the work.

I was aged 31. This new business involved establishing another optician's shop but this time embracing technical work which I had planned to include to make our service more extensive than in my first Littlehampton enterprise.

Somehow the word got around that I had moved back to London and the minister from the local church came to see me, as did ministers from other denominations who made a habit of calling in. The topic of conversation was often about the New Theology as advanced by Reginald John Campbell, who was a British Congregationalist and Anglican divine who became a popular preacher while he was the minister at the London City Temple. He was a leading exponent of the 'New Theology' movement of 1907. (As far as I could ascertain, Campbell never had a spiritual experience or direct revelation himself and seemed to rely on the experience of others to form his views.)

These experiences, however, showed the way my own spiritual work would develop in the future.

At first, we lived in London but soon moved to a little cottage just outside and in the country which had a large garden. I was able to travel by bicycle to and from the business and home. (London was much smaller then, compared to 1947 as I write this.) My wife and I would go for long walks in the country and would often stop off at a café/roadhouse to enjoy teas, strawberries and almost any food you might desire; it was many years before rationing became commonplace.

It was at this stage of my life that I became known as a Food Reform fanatic. I never could do things by halves and, as usual, went to extremes. Not being satisfied with conducting experiments on myself to reduce my weight from around 170lbs to 130lbs, I pushed my reform ideas onto others by giving lectures here, there and everywhere. The message I was advancing was that if we eat pure food, we think pure thoughts, and live pure lives and so bring in an age of harmony and peace.

I clearly believed it myself, and some of those I lectured to also believed it. However, it did not meet our expectations, or deliver the promises put forward in the many books I drew upon for inspiration and information. Eating pure food did not make us think pure thoughts or live pure lives. My experience showed that I had been putting the cart before the horse, and that the first thing necessary was a change of thought, after which other things would follow as a matter of course.

I was then and still am a non-flesh eater.

The fact that I clutched at this straw of an idea, vainly as it proved, to live a pure life, showed that there was a desire in my heart to live such a life. It was not until later that I understood the need to focus on just the thought process as the principal action, and this was to be the later and most meaningful part of my life's work. At the time of writing, I have been trying to pass on this reality of the power of thought for 26 years. *(Author's note: HTH was to complete 37 years devoted to this task.)*

It was at this juncture that our first child was born. The *London Evening News*, commenting on the fact that he was the child of Fruitarian parents, and born at a Fruitarian nursing home, suggested respectfully that our son and heir should be given the name of "Little Pip". Unsurprisingly, we did not adopt this suggestion.

At about the same time, I noticed an advertisement for books dealing with an idea called "New Thought". The advertisement claimed that our thinking was responsible for everything which comes into our lives; I ordered some and thought I would try out the advice.

These books put into words several ideas that had been on my mind for some time. Having a practical mindset, I determined to put the teaching into practice to ascertain whether it worked at all. The books may have had beautiful words and idealistic ideas, but I had to assess whether the system advocated worked.

I did my best to follow the guidance given and this resulted in a demand by me on the Infinite, God. As, by now, I had expanded my

London activity and was operating several other optician businesses on the same lines as my first, again without any capital, my desire was to increase the general level of business and hence money taken in. Thus, I decided to demand from the Infinite, God, in the way these books advocated.

As a result, every night I went down to the bottom of the garden and offered up my prayers to God, with great determination and sincerity. I would repeat the process regularly and then I would wait anxiously for the results. Each week I was disappointed that the level of business in my various branches remained steady, sometimes up a little and at others down but there was no sign that my requests were being answered; in fact, I felt that they had not even been heard.

However, I persevered, but things went from bad to worse, until at last I decided to call all my creditors together. The upshot was not totally negative in that they allowed me to continue trading, but at a lower level than I had previously aspired to.

This was a challenging time, but, as I look at it now, it triggered the foundation of my later life of producing *The Science of Thought Review*.

It was soon after this that our second son was born. Little did we know it at the time, for God mercifully withholds the future from us, that this dear son would be with us for a short time. It was to be through him that we would receive the greatest blow that life dealt us.

But we must all experience sorrows as well as joys, for life is made up of sunshine and shadow, light and shade.

We start life with never a negative thought and are eager to go forward and see everything with the unblemished eyes of youth. But as we journey through life, we encounter obstacles and sorrow until in old age we are content to remain alive and be patient. At that juncture, we no longer look forward, for there is nothing more to look forward to and by then we know not to dwell too much on the past except to appreciate the good things that God has led us towards. So, in old age, we live in the present, knowing that God and the present moment are sufficient.

Although by now I felt that I had the businesses under control, I had a recurrence of a feeling of restlessness and a constant urge to live away from London in the heart of the country. I envisaged living outside the big metropolis and travelling to and from work. Thus, we found a pleasant house on the Sussex/Hampshire border with an acre of garden. I travelled home for long weekends, from Friday to Monday.

This arrangement worked well for a time, but the amount of labour involved in looking after an acre of garden must be experienced to be believed. Inevitably, we employed a gardener, and found that the expense of this, together with that of travelling to and from work each week, made moving back nearer to London a more sensible arrangement. And after a year or two we moved back to a house that was still in the country but only two or three miles from my businesses, of which there were now several branches. This was more convenient for us all. (This was, of course, well before the huge expansion of London in the 1920s and 1930s.)

But still I cherished a deep love of the country, and this is a feeling I had had all my life. Inevitably, I deduced that I would not be able to meet this aspiration until I was able to retire from business altogether. I knew that I was not in business for the love of it, although I was stimulated by it, but saw it as a means to an end. Deep down I knew that I had to return to the country, and I sensed, only vaguely, the type of work I might do when I was finally settled there. However, I had no realisation then of what this future work might entail.

But again, life was beckoning, and I felt called to make yet another change in my occupation.

Looking back on it all now, it does not seem to me that I was daring or enterprising but, rather, I was being carried along on the crest of a wave of my own creation.

I had been making strong demands on God, which at the time seemed only to make matters worse, but they were eventually to bear fruit in the form of a major change in my life and occupation. This next change was to make every enterprise that had gone before appear trivial in comparison with what lay ahead.

And I still had the strong urges of my childhood when I vowed that I would climb out of the rut of respectable poverty into which I had been born. As mentioned before, I had also been inspired by books I had read earlier telling the stories of those who themselves had climbed out of poverty to greatness, and these set my imagination alight. I knew by now that imagination is perhaps the greatest power we possess. But one had to be careful, because going in the wrong direction could lead to suffering and possible disaster, whereas going in a right direction could bring true achievement and many blessings.

But it is quite clear to me now, as I write this many years later, that my imagination was set on material achievement and that this would lead to suffering. We reap what we have sown.

If, when we are young, our imagination is fired with ambition to achieve great things, there would appear to be a sort of tidal wave of power built up that can sweep us along towards our imagined objective. It seems to me that we can realise the objectives from our imagination. This links to the idea that the Lamas of Tibet can build up an entity of power that accompanies them wherever they go. But I am not able to say more about this.

What I can say, however, is that this is how I have found things work but clearly there will be contrary views. Some people may think that God has a fixed plan for everyone, but my belief is that we have the free will to follow our imagination.

But for me there was a new enterprise looming....

If we would only trust God more and make greater and more daring ventures in faith, then it would not be necessary for us to be driven by life's experiences to the end of our tether.

God's Sustaining Grace

HT Hamblin

Chapter 12

An Adventure in the West End

This next great change in my life came about quite by accident, or so it seemed. I was asked to do some specialist optical work in the West End of London. This led to more demand in the same area and before long, I found myself deeply involved in this new enterprise. I had not sought this work, but it was thrust on me.

These new tasks required me to work doubly hard with half a day spent in the West End and the rest of the day at my normal businesses. This necessitated working very late at night, so late sometimes that I missed the last train home and had to walk the three miles instead. By the time I reached home on these occasions I was so fatigued that all I could do was collapse into a chair in a state of complete exhaustion. Clearly, I was overworked. And I exacerbated the situation in that I did not make time for proper meals and existed only on snacks.

Consequently, I went downhill fast and before long became so weak that I could hardly think. But I struggled on. I have no idea how I managed but I kept going until August 1909, at which juncture I was offered a good price for the several existing London businesses, which I accepted. This closed another chapter of my life.

Clearly, I needed to recuperate and my wife, our two children and I went back to our beloved East Anglia to spend time at our favourite haunts.

It only required a few weeks of this for my health to become fully restored, at which point we returned to our home just outside London. I was then again approached by my clients in the West End and knew that I had some serious thinking to do as to whether I pursued this new opportunity.

I was not at all keen on starting this fresh venture. Now that I had some capital behind me from the sale of the previous businesses, I could afford to be selective. In the back of my mind, I knew that I would prefer to have an enterprise based in the country where conditions were less exacting than in London.

But my line of thinking did not meet with the approval of those who had brought me to the West End in the first place. They wanted to use my services as I was offering more than my competitors.

They said that I really *must* start and that, if I did so, my success would be assured and that I would soon have as much business as I could manage. One of these individuals even said to me: "I've found the ideal premises for you, come with me, and let us go and look".

So, we went and had a look. It was indeed an excellent place, and I was persuaded to go and see the solicitor, who was managing the letting, immediately. This was on a Thursday and my thinking was that if I took the lease, I should aim to be open for business the following Monday. This was a very tight schedule, but I really did not care whether I took the place or not. I suspect that the solicitor detected my attitude and he probably feared that he might "lose" a possible let. Clearly my disinterest worked, as after about half-an-hour's negotiation, I left his office with the key to the new premises in my pocket. In addition, the solicitor granted me a 21-year lease without a premium. And all this despite my being almost unknown and without having any written references to show him.

I had Friday and Saturday to fit the place up, furnish it, etc, ready to receive clients on Monday morning. By Saturday evening everything was ready.

I called the business Theodore Hamblin Limited.

When I arrived on Monday morning, I was surprised to see that there was already a client waiting to see me. He was the head of a large Canadian concern and would remain a loyal customer throughout my time in the business and even after I had retired from it.

I regarded this new enterprise as my last great gamble, if it failed, I would be irretrievably lost, whereas if it succeeded, I would become a wealthy man. In the latter case there would, of course, be no need for any further gambles.

The premises were at 15 Wigmore Street, Cavendish Square, London.

This new venture, according to conventional worldly wisdom and business standards, was doomed to failure. Some people said that I would be finished in six months whilst others said just three months. Their reasons were probably based on their own knowledge of the West End of London which they reminded me was the most conservative place in the world for business. It was said that until a firm has been established for many years, most people will not even recognise its existence. I was told several times that it takes almost unlimited capital, time, and patience just to gain a footing in what was then probably the most exclusive market in the world.

However, I had two things in my favour. First was the incredibly low rent with the very long lease which I had secured for the premises. Second, my work was known to a few influential people who seemed to be even more enthusiastic about the potential for the business than I was and would surely encourage other people to come to me.

The gamble came off, although it was a challenge as I was operating on extended credit terms from my suppliers and, initially, taking in only modest sums. It was, of course, necessary for me to work very long hours, although solvency was never a serious issue as I was receiving small but regular payments from a firm which owed me money and this was a useful cushion in the first weeks.

Although this account may read as a touch-and-go story, the business was a success from the very first day. At the end of this first day, I found that I had done enough business to pay all expenses for the first week and make a small profit. I took very little money home myself and my wife never complained. She knew, of course, that I was ploughing profits into the business to build up a decent funding reserve.

At the end of the first day, I felt triumphant, and the feeling reminded me of my first ever day at school where I returned home and proudly told my mother that I had learnt about "pot hooks and hangers".

It was soon after I started this new business that I had a recurrence of an awareness of God being very close, which I have earlier referred to as The Presence. It was at the end of a long day at work, and I was tired and took a short rest in my revolving office reclining chair which gave me a view to the west through a large window part-glazed with chlorophyll coloured glass giving a pleasing light.

I have always found light filtered through such glass to be restful, but on this occasion, the effect was far greater than anything I had previously experienced. It seemed to me that I was leaning back, not on a reclining chair, but on what felt like an embrace by the Infinite in the form of another visit by the Presence; the same type of feeling I had at my Baptism. It was a very powerful sensation.

I felt that, at last and after many years of struggle, I was perfectly comfortable, perfectly fitted into my environment, perfectly at one with the pattern of life and surrounded by an all-pervading feeling of the spiritual Essence. It is this spiritual Essence which underpins the whole universe. It is God.

For a moment, I knew then that I was a true child of the Eternal, of God. I felt no emotion, no rapture, no ecstasy, but only a sense of great comfort and certainty. Fear was completely absent. I knew that I was in my right place as part of the Cosmic Whole, this being the cosmic body made of all the atoms, space, and light in nature, with God as its centre. I was at peace.

This experience lasted only a minute or two, maybe five, but it made a great impression on me. I interpreted it at the time to mean that good fortune was coming to me and, if phenomenal business success can be termed good fortune, then my interpretation was correct.

However, I had not yet learnt that the greatest financial success can be the greatest failure in terms of personal well-being. To me in those years, business was more of a game than a serious task. I enjoyed the thrill of developing it and saw it as an adventure but, once it was established and making money, it ceased to interest me. The fact that I had worked like a galley slave and given some of the best years of my life to creating the enterprise were forgotten. In fact, I lost interest.

My mother's prediction that I was 'unstable as water and would not excel' did not seem to be working out as predicted. I was a determined individual and would suffer anything to make my work a success. It was only when this had been achieved that I began to feel an urge for change; and only after all the hard, pioneering, work had been done would my interest wane. I just did not enjoy the monotony of reaping where I had sown, as it lacked the excitement of creating a new venture. I suppose I was attracted to the excitement of fighting apparently lost causes.

Those with a pioneering spirit are often the same, it seems, whereas other people are content to reap where they and others have sown.

The business was a most amazing success and it increased by leaps and bounds, and it was only with the greatest difficulty that I and my staff were able to manage its rapid expansion. One of the problems we encountered was with the number of motor cars in which customers travelled to us; this was in the very early days of motorised vehicles. The streets of London in those days were congested not just with motor cars but from a combination of horse-drawn vehicles, omnibuses and people who preferred to walk on the road rather than the pavements.

We had to employ a commissionaire to open and shut car doors of visiting vehicles, regulate traffic, and arrange the parking of our customers' vehicles in a side street.

With success seemingly assured, I was approached by the landlord's solicitor again with the offer of extending to a forty-two-year lease on the whole building on highly favourable terms. Naturally I accepted it, especially as it ensured that the rent payable was reduced to almost negligible proportions.

Everything seemed to be going my way. I did not have to solicit new business and instead, business came seeking me.

It was not only the rich and powerful who came but many interesting people, explorers, politicians, judges, and their respective wives. For example, I remember Mrs Asquith, the wife of the then Prime Minister, not only as a customer but as a friendly and witty conversationalist.

Their personal demands on my services were very exacting. The great ones did not like having to wait their turn, but wait they had to. I remember one important lady, a Duchess, who, on entering my office, flounced herself down to utter a somewhat heated remark: "Really, Mr Hamblin, you are as difficult to see as the first surgeon in Europe".

And that was one of my troubles. Although I had a large and well-trained staff of assistants, the demands on my personal service were so exacting that I felt as though I had become a slave.

If I'd had the time to reflect, I might have thought about those early times when I made strong demands in my prayers. Reflection might have brought me to the conclusion that I had overdone my demands and that it would have been better had I been more moderate in my requests. Also, I concluded that it would have been wiser had I requested some of the better things of life, things which are so precious that money cannot buy them, such as harmony, happiness, contentment, health, etc. But I was where I was!

I had my first encounter with royalty a few months after opening the new business with a summons to Buckingham Palace to be interviewed by a senior member of the Palace staff. This I duly did and was informed that I would be required to work for a Royal Princess and would be summoned in due course. With a request like this I accepted of course and, feeling elated, walked back to my business feeling light on my feet. Things were indeed coming my way.

But when the time came for my visit to the Palace to see the Princess, I did not feel at all lifted-up or elated. Instead, I felt very nervous and wondered how a one-time poor boy, with almost no education, would perform in the forthcoming interview. I knew that I had discarded my uncultured way of speaking and that I could speak standard English without accent or affection, but I was nervous about meeting someone at the very pinnacle of society. On the positive side, I knew that my manner of talking to my clients was highly successful, although I remained nervous about my lowly origin becoming an issue.

The appointed day arrived. I went to the Palace by taxi, and everything went well. In fact, at the end of the interview, as if to show her innate friendliness and complete absence of superiority or snobbishness, the Royal Princess held out her hand and gave me a warm handshake. Then I opened the door for her, made a bow as well as I could, which was graciously acknowledged, and that was the end of my first experience with royalty.

On return to my taxi, or more correctly somebody else's taxi as mine had been commandeered by a Duke, I thought to myself how quickly I was going up in the world. Then I thought that rockets go up very quickly, but they also come down just as fast, or even faster, than they went up. And when they hit the ground, they break up into pieces. "Better be careful Henry", I said to myself.

But my life was in safer hands than mine.

Although I continued to ascend in the world of business, socially we remained much the same. Indeed, for several years we lived in the same small house which we were occupying when the new business began.

In 1910 our third child was born, this time a daughter.

In the summer of 1911, a great heatwave descended on the country and in London the day-time maximum rose steadily to reach 100deg Fahrenheit in the shade. The great heat, coupled with bad milk, brought our little daughter almost to death's door and we had to escape.

I was fortunate that we were all able to escape to the East Coast, where the temperature was only 75 degrees Fahrenheit and the milk arrived each day fresh and pure. This move undoubtably saved our daughter's life.

This move to the coast was a great relief to me as well and enabled me to tolerate the heatwave, which was greater than I had ever experienced before, or since.

I was not the only one who found life difficult under such conditions, and this reminds me of a visit I received from an Indian Prince during this great heat before we had escaped to East Anglia. He was a diplomat on duty in London and felt it necessary to wear a full frock coat suit and, of course, a turban. He said that the intense heat made him feel ill and he feared he might collapse from it at any moment. When I suggested to him that the heat was even greater in his country, he explained that their buildings were built to withstand the heat, that the punkahs are always at work, and, he added, they wore the thinnest of silk clothes. "But here," he continued, "your buildings and streets are not built to withstand heat, there are no punkahs, and, unfortunately, I have to wear these dreadful thick clothes."

He went away without collapsing, but I was intrigued to know why a native of India felt as though he was dying in *our* heat. That was how I felt too, but at least I could discard my usual heavy jacket and roll up my shirtsleeves and was not encumbered by a heavy frock coat.

It was in 1912 that I bought my first motor car and learnt to drive it; in those days private cars were little more than a novelty and there were very few on the road. Driving was less exacting than it is today as I write this in 1947. We used it to travel on holiday to the East Coast rather than go by rail; it was a very simple vehicle and not grand in any way.

Later I used to leave my wife and family at our holiday home and afford myself the luxury of travelling to London each Monday and back on the Friday and having meals on the train. This was a new experience for me as, for all my life, I had never been able to afford such things. Although my feeling of satisfaction at my new status did not last long, it was an experience I would not have missed.

My wife and I and our family lived a simple life. We bought no fine clothes and we both hated finery and ostentation, but at least we no longer had to pinch and scrape. I had climbed out of the "rut of circumstance" into which I had been born and this gave me satisfaction; but it did not bring happiness. I pondered this and even thought wistfully of the earlier times when we had to pinch and scrape and meet financial crises with nothing but our faith the sustain us.

Somehow, I felt that they were happier times.

All my life I had striven to get on in the world and yet, now that this had been accomplished, I could see nothing to appeal in the future. All I had to do was to go on as I was and become as rich and powerful as I wanted. But this repelled me as it would spell the end of the simple life both my wife and I loved to lead. It would mean, instead, entering a new servitude, the servitude of the rich and well-to-do, who know little true happiness or peace but just the continual pursuit of wealth. Always having to do something to fill the emptiness in their hearts.

"*For what shall it profit a man if he gain the whole world and lose his own soul*"? (Mark 8 v 36).

Had I struggled all these years, and worn myself out, only for this?

The magic key to the Inner Kingdom is simply Love.

The Way of the Practical Mystic

HT Hamblin

Chapter 13

Thus Far Shalt Thou Go

We often read in the Bible of the men of old being warned by God in a dream. He still warns us in similar ways, although the detail may differ. It may be that these experiences, which were called dreams in the Bible, were more like visions in the night. Some people today have such experiences which may have brought them consolation, but I never have, although my wife has.

Like many people, I have had vivid dreams at times, but they have normally had a farcical character with disconnected and jumbled-up ideas. Once, however, I had a pre-vision dream which turned out to be true in every detail, and it has been the only one of its kind I have had.

It happened as follows. I had been having a problem with one of my ears and the doctors decided that I should undergo a small operation to resolve the issue. It required me to have a general anaesthetic with the procedure being executed in a local nursing home. After it was done, I woke up sufficiently to recognise the surgeon, and then I went into a deep sleep which lasted until the morning.

During this deep sleep I dreamt with clarity that the morning had arrived and that the nurse had come to take my temperature. In my dream I saw her take a thermometer from its container and then shake it to force the mercury to the bottom of the tube. To my surprise, as soon as she shook it, the mercury end disappeared. This dream made a great impression on me and the memory of it remains vivid today.

But the really striking event was early the next morning when the "real" nurse appeared to take my temperature. She produced a thermometer and shook it, and then, just as I had seen in my dream, the mercury end disappeared. "How strange," I exclaimed, "that is precisely what I saw in my dream". So, to appease her curiosity, I told her exactly what I had dreamt, at which she was astonished and went to get a replacement thermometer and tell the Matron of my strange dream. On hearing the story, the Matron came to see me and said that I must be psychic. But I know that I am not psychic.

I attributed the remarkable dream to the drugs I had been given to make me sleep. In neither the dream nor the actual event did I see what caused the thermometer to break but I certainly saw very clearly the result of the shaking.

This was not the only strange experience I had whilst I was in full swing building up my business in the West End and when my mind was totally given to that task. I spared no time then to think of higher things.

The dream pattern experienced was generally the same. I would awake in the night with a feeling that I was in Hell. I do not use that word as a figure of speech but in its literal sense; I felt that I was in the place of the doomed. I felt as though I was looking back over a past which covered the history of man and included all the hopeless despair of the doomed of all ages. I could also sense the lamentations of the doomed, and their hopeless despair, and felt as though it was all concentrated in my own soul. If I thought of the future, it made me shudder. All the sorrow, the despair, the hopelessness of a lost humanity seemed to be poured into me. It was as though I was in a bottomless pit.

These dreams followed the same general pattern each time and I find it impossible to describe them accurately in words, but I remember them as indescribably awful.

Strangely, I would emerge from each dream into consciousness for a few moments and then go to sleep again and in the morning, I would endeavour to forget each one, although I could not completely shake off the memory, and was perturbed whenever these dreams occurred.

My solution was to devote even more of my energy to the business and it was almost like a therapy to realise that I had started with practically nothing and worked my way up through overwhelming difficulties. To me it was an all-engrossing sport and its stimulus helped me to forget the solemn warning the messages of my dreams had been giving me. Overall, I was as disturbed as ever by my focus on material things as all my thoughts had been about the business and I never spared the time for even a thought for the spiritual and higher dimensions of life.

These experiences were there as a warning to me.

Then came another and quite different warning. It was a warning of forthcoming world upheaval. This did not come in any subjective sense or from a dream but from one of my clients, an American Congressman.

We had a long conversation, and he was clearly an admirer of my country. But he suddenly shocked me by saying: "there is one thing that I feel very sorry about, and that is that you are not getting ready for your war with Germany". This was in 1913. I was a bit startled by his remark and replied: "But we are not going to war with Germany; we want to be friends. Live and let live is the wish of our people as far as the man in the street is concerned".

His response was that it was not in our hands. He said: "Germany is arming to the teeth and straining every effort with the aim of defeating the British nation, once and for all". He added that other countries appreciated only too clearly what was afoot and that it was only in Britain that people were so blind.

This clear insight by such a person, and expressed with such clarity that it was almost callous, gave me a shock. What was to become of us all if we were invaded? At the time it was all very disturbing.

But clearly, I shook off the warning and instead went ahead with schemes for the business that were expensive and with which I would not have progressed had I really believed that war would break out within a year of our meeting.

Meanwhile, my own life was heading towards another crisis although I was not aware of it at the time. All I was aware of at my inner level was an increasing dissatisfaction and sense of frustration and futility in my life.

My principal concern was that the business was becoming far larger than I wanted. I had intended it to be successful and remunerative but had never wanted it to become so large that I could not handle it comfortably. Now I found I was powerless to stop its growth. It was rather like a H.G. Wells' character, the boy who was fed on a particular food such that he grew and continued to do so until he was so tall that ordinary people looked like pygmies. Once his growth started, nothing could stop it. It was the same with my business. It had attained a momentum of its own; I had created a monster which was now my master. Not only had I created a major ophthalmic company but was also engaged in designing and manufacturing a wide range of optical equipment.

Could I ever break free?

I was reaping where I had sown and was beginning to see the effect of my own thoughts and imagination projected in my prayers, especially in my earlier years, when I was determined to climb out of my poverty-trap. I was beginning to see the result of desires focused on a specific goal and how they can release invisible powers that may not be fulfilled until years after they are set in motion.

Do not be deceived: God is not mocked, for whatever one sows, that will he also reap. (Galatians 6:7)

I had started on a slippery slope down which I was accelerating. If nothing could stop me, my inner ruin would be complete. I could see myself being a rich man but hemmed in on every side by wealth and its responsibilities and, metaphorically, hardly able to breathe. I envisaged being finished off by a heart attack or stroke and buried at a comparatively early age, with pomp and ceremony. I did not like this thought; the outlook seemed to me to be appalling.

Where were my dreams of freedom and a life lived near to Nature? Of seeing the sun rise, of walking barefoot on the early morning dew? Of making friends with every living being? Were they gone forever? It seemed so.

Infrequently, I could find time to take my wife and children to a local quiet beauty spot but, once there, I found I could no longer appreciate it. My finer senses had become so blunted and coarsened that I could no longer respond to Nature's gentle call. I have found that Nature can be appreciated fully only by those who are attuned to her moods; alas, I was out of tune. As far as Nature was concerned, I was an outcast. And I had brought this on myself from concentrating on material success to the exclusion of everything else.

I had indeed achieved success, but was being compelled to pay a very high price.

I remembered then something my father told me during a visit; it was after my mother had died, and he said: "Dear mother visited me in a vision in the night; not an ordinary dream because she appeared as plainly and distinctly as when she was alive". This sounded like the same sort of experience I had had.

On another occasion, when I was visiting him, he decided to have one of his dozes and, when he awoke, said to me: "I am told that you are paying too heavy a price for success". Of course, I responded that everything was satisfactory. The reality was that my father knew absolutely nothing about my business enterprise. This comment of his perturbed me; how did he know what I was already beginning to sense in my own mind?

My father's remarks about his dreams, together with my own powerful ones, increased my uneasiness, which was already well established; I was troubled.

With my finer sensitivities already blunted by my huge focus on business, I remember my wife once telling me that the best wool came from sheep which grazed on the high pastures, whereas those that lived in the valleys, where conditions were benign, produced lower quality wool.

I reflected on this and wondered if a similar analogy applied to people. If we live on a mountain top and breathe the finer airs of Heavenly thought, our senses become attuned to the finer aspects of life. My own life was akin to that of a sheep which had been brought down to the valley for grazing; I had been coarsened by it and my finer sensibilities blunted in that I had become an outcast from both Nature and God. It was of my own making.

I can see this so clearly now and realise that I got myself into this position from my selfishness but, deep down, I knew that God's love was still there to welcome me back.

But could I go back? I had created something which would not stop and from which I could not readily escape.

However, God had something better in store for me than to become a rich and miserable man, although I did not realise this at the time. Even if I had been told this in those years, I would not have believed it and would probably have reacted with derision.

There was, however, one very positive outcome from my new-found wealth in that I had an opportunity to begin to appreciate fine music. Previously, I had regarded classical music as merely discordant noise and in this I was a thorough-going philistine. However, encouraged by my wife, I had purchased a player-piano (pianola), and I well remember playing the *Moonlight Sonata* on the machine and was soon enthralled by the music. And when I later heard the same music played again in a recital, I was captivated.

I learnt that the difference between imitation and the real thing is so great that the former is just a ghostly echo of the latter. I saw a parallel in our own lives with the pursuit of worldly things compared to spiritual ones.

Another aspect of my changed circumstances was that, although I could continue living a rather frugal life if I preferred, I did not have to, as money was no longer an issue. It was a matter of personal choice. When eating a simple meal of bread and cheese from choice, rather than enjoying a three-course meal for which we could pay without even noticing the cost, the simplicity of the frugal meal brings its own satisfaction.

Those who have never been comfortably off financially, quite naturally but mistakenly in my experience, think that if they enjoyed a larger income, they would be happier. My experience is that the reverse is more generally the case. A larger income provides more opportunity to acquire houses and things that, of themselves, can lead to additional responsibilities and stress.

My experience has shown me that the only way to be cured of this deep-seated delusion is to get on with life and find out the truth of the matter for yourself. I have found that having more possessions and living more expensively does not, of itself, bring contentment.

The late Bramwell Booth, a British charity worker who was the first Chief of Staff of the Salvation Army and later the General of The Salvation Army, after his father, tells of the story of travelling with Cecil Rhodes, the South African millionaire, in a South African train. On an impulse, Bramwell leaned forward and asked, "Are you happy, Mr Rhodes?" Rhodes looked astonished and answered candidly, "Happy? Why good Lord, no". He spoke as though he knew that wealth, far from bringing happiness, can often drive it away.

Wealth makes it possible to indulge in all forms of activity and sensation. But my experience is that for every indulgence we undertake we can attract a level of suffering, and therefore I believe that an austere way of life is beneficial. But I certainly do not believe that austerity should be taken to an extreme where the cure becomes worse than the problem.

The middle path is the path of Wisdom.

Visualising is the true creative faculty of the mind... If the mind concentrates on it perfectly, all the invisible forces of life work together in such a way as to reproduce the ideal in our outward life. Vision always precedes achievement.

HT Hamblin

Chapter 14

I Retire from the Scene

One of my difficulties had always been my unreliable and often poor state of health and for many years I was scarcely free of pain; no one else knew about it except the doctors I consulted in Harley Street. Although they wrote a lot of things down in books, they were unable to identify the cause of my trouble and, of more concern, they could not suggest any remedy.

London fogs were frequent in the early 1900s and this was because the London air was heavily polluted, as coal, coke or wood was the only way a house could be heated, and this was by using open fires. There was no other way of heating a house then and certainly there was no central heating.

These fogs nearly asphyxiated me and each winter I would contract severe colds which followed one after another. They were so bad that often I felt more like dying than going to the business, and, when I was at work, it required all the determination I could muster to attend to my clients and give them the best possible service.

Certainly, the air quality in those days was not ideal for me.

Also, I relied on hasty snacks instead of proper meals, and I had irregular times for feeding. Unsurprisingly, this brought me into a nervous condition which was a challenge not only for me but for my staff.

However, there was now an added cause of illness. With my inner conflict between the business pulling me one way and my desire to live an entirely different life which was pulling in another direction, I began to suffer from a degree of psychological illness. Moreover, throughout this time my night experiences continued to trouble me, and I often found myself waking up in the night amidst lamentations of Hell and the despair of thousands of people which were all centred on me, or so it seemed. I felt again that I was suffering everything that the doomed of all ages had ever suffered. I looked down the long vista of my wasted years and felt despair, remorse, regret, and hopelessness.

These unpleasant night experiences continued until I had firmly made up my mind to retire from business altogether. As soon as I had declared my decision they ceased completely. I can only assume that the dreams stopped because whatever was triggering them had achieved its object. I surmise that they were sent to warn me that I was travelling on the wrong road for my life, and that God had something different in store for me.

I was probably suffering from some sort of stress accumulation coupled with a poor diet, but I was certainly not happy with the prospect of having to keep on working at high intensity while the good things of life were being neglected. I did not even have the requisite time to contribute in person to my family, as I was a slave to my business. My thoughts ran on the lines that I could not bear to think of the future, and of the consequences of continuing to live in the way I was, and possibly dying young whilst at work. It was like being in a prison.

There was nothing for me to look forward to. I did not want to do any of the conventional activities which rich people often do. I could see no pleasure in playing golf, or hunting, or yachting, or being a member of a club, or in public dinners, or in feasting on rich food, or drinking expensive drinks, or wearing smart clothes. Neither did I want to travel and visit many places and, to be honest, I disliked just the thought of it.

Thoughts of the older days came back to me. Of the time spent sharing a cottage with an agricultural labourer and his wife; of the time I was allowed to take my spell at a plough, of admiring the way my friend could communicate with the horses pulling the plough, of the straight and true furrows we occasionally produced, and which were so pleasing to the eye and satisfying to the soul.

And the conflict went on. There seemed to be a state of continued hostility between me as a man of business, who delighted in the rough and tumble of competition, and the other me as a lover of country and as a would-be mystic. It was like a tug of war with me in a permanent position of "taking the strain".

Unsurprisingly, no one could understand me and I was indeed a strange case. People said behind my back: "Why cannot he be happy and contented as other people would be if in his position?" Here was I with the ball at my feet, with everything going my way, with everything for which many people strived and would sell their souls. And yet, even then, I was unhappy and did not even want to remain long enough to collect the metaphorical fruits off the trees.

Even in the early years with the West End business when life seemed so rewarding, I knew that I was being called to do other things in life. I knew, deep down, that I would find no rest until I obeyed the call.

But there were other conflicts in my mind. Was I running away from a difficult situation just to live an easier life? Was what I was thinking of doing merely an act of cowardice? Was I afraid to face the responsibility of the life I had won for myself? Was I run down and weak from nervous exhaustion? Was I seeking to escape and retire to a religious institution like some who wish to escape from the world?

I had known of such cases of escape. Men who had been in

prominent positions in the world, and who were talked about, attacked, supported, hated by some loved by others, and the very centre of attention and interest. They got over-stressed, their health failed, and then they gave up the struggle and were tired of fighting alone and eventually entered a retreat or similar organisation and were never heard of again.

I did not want to be like them.

I knew it would not be wise to decide on my future with the business whilst I was feeling ill and run down and that such important decisions should only be made when one is fit and well. But I knew that I was not fit and well. I knew too that I was facing the biggest decision of my life and yet I felt that I had to make this decision soon and before my health failed further.

But how could I get out of business if I did decide to retire? It was a young business and only a few years old and still depended on my personality to a large extent. And, if I retired, who would then run it? Life just seemed to be all problems.

Then I appreciated that I needed to respect those who had given me support through thick and thin. What about their feelings if I turned my back on all their kindness? After all they had done for me, this would be a display of the deepest ingratitude. I felt trapped.

However, the decision was forced on me by a further deterioration of health which I was powerless to overcome. My nervous condition had also got so bad that I was unable to write legibly and was not in a fit state to meet my many clients.

By now the business had two other directors who, with me together with the Company Secretary, made up the Board.

It was agreed by all that a compromise was required. The result was an agreement under which I would retire from active participation in the business but would remain the Chairman of the two limited companies which now comprised the business. I would attend monthly Board Meetings and be available at other times for advice and consultation, as required.

This settlement was not reached without a bit of a struggle with the medical fraternity. The two most respected physicians in London at the time inspected and tested me and held earnest consultations about me. One concluded that life on a farm was the only thing that would restore me to health. The other thought that I might be able to carry on with the business if I was able to work undisturbed in a sound-proof room away from the telephones and bustle of the business in the same way that he worked with his patients, in a quiet room free from interruptions.

Of course, the latter suggestion was out of the question and ignored the fact that I did not want to carry on. I knew I was past it and said so. I went on to say that if they did not allow me to get away from it all and into the country, I could do something desperate. I made it clear that, as far as I was concerned, I was at the end of my tether.

After that, there was not much more to be said.

I left the business under the two directors who had joined in the past year or so, and their energetic management ensured that it developed enormously and well beyond anything I could have realised. It was all due to their untiring efforts and enterprise that this was achieved. I was never in favour of big expansion, preferring to have a business of reasonable proportions which I could manage comfortably, and I could never have achieved what they did. I realise now that I was not cut out for big business.

Looking back on my life it seems at first to have been a wasted effort. Not one of the things I took up ever led to anything since in every case I went off at a tangent leaving others to reap where I had sown. But I can see now that my efforts were not completely wasted. There was a certain method to my apparent madness, although I was ignorant of it at the time. I now see that my first occupation was a good preparation for the second. My first work was a good training in hand and eye co-ordination which stood me in good stead for all later work. It was the third business that grew so much that it exhausted me.

The only formal training I received was at the work bench after leaving school and, after that, all my later enterprises required me to be self-taught.

If this book is being read by a young reader who is still at school, I must stress that you should not follow my example. I have been hampered in my life by a lack of education and qualifications although it happened to work out successfully in my case. Today, however, the chances of an individual achieving success without a backing of good education are much less than I encountered. Thus, my advice to young people is to take education seriously as your future life will depend on it.

But education is not everything and there needs to be more than just learning. One may possess determination, perseverance, courage and more but I believe there is something else needed by a successful individual. What this "something" might be is difficult to describe but is a form of secular spiritual power which is a power that can carry one through difficult challenges where others, possibly more gifted in their qualifications, may fail. It is not just "head learning" that counts.

My own life has seen me change occupations many times with each change being a step upwards. But I do not recommend this; moderation in all things and a less radical approach is a better way. In my own case my final occupation was as a writer, and I have often wondered how many other people found themselves in my position as they moved into the years when retirement would be the norm.

However, despite my remarks about career changes, I would not discourage those who feel that they must make a change, or even several. If change is their ambition, they will never achieve fulfilment unless they follow their inclinations. A distinction must be made, however, between wanting to make a change simply through lack of perseverance, or some weakness, as compared to an ambition to take on new challenges. If one feels that one phase of life is ending, perhaps by outgrowing the occupation, and that one has the ability, enthusiasm, and energy to make a change, then certainly I think that should be done.

It may mean a level of risk, but it can result in great benefits.

Back to my West End business. At last, the day arrived when I would no longer be travelling to London every day from our house just outside London and, although situated on top of a hill, it was not what I would call real country. There was too much of the suburb about it, although it gave me my first opportunity to become a spectator at several sporting events and I even had a strange liking for watching cricket matches.

Having effectively retired I found time to help in the local community and almost immediately became involved in minor building works requiring hard labour on my part. But my dear loyal wife had misgivings about this and took the view that if I was well enough to do that sort of heavy work then I should be well enough to look after my own business instead of leaving it to others, with the potential risk that they might fritter away what I had built up.

But of course, a change of occupation can be one of the best restoratives and can quickly help one overcome the symptoms of being overwrought as I most certainly was. I have always found that the mind can be reset by undertaking mechanical work and one of my favourites was to dismantle a clock, clean the parts, and then put them all back together again. I invariably found that by the time I had completed my task the tension I felt in my mind had reverted to normal. I was not alone in this and knew someone who, when mentally ill due to overwork and worry, would take time off from his normal work to build a new clock from scratch. By the time he had completed building one, he would be fully recovered.

As my own health steadily improved, I, together with my wife, began to think about moving into what I called the real country. We became regular readers of magazines like The Field with a view to seeing what houses were available on the market. But those advertised were all too grand for us as we envisaged something more modest.

We took the car and went south, first into Hampshire and then into West Sussex. At Bosham we found a good-looking house with about 3 acres of ground with open country on all four sides. Also, the sea came almost to a stone's throw of the house at high tide; it was not the open sea but a branch of Chichester Harbour. The house was, and still is, called Kenwood.

It had other attractions too. There was a well-built coach house with stables which were used as a coal house. (In those days we could fill it with the best coal at not much more than one pound per ton.) Also, there was an artesian well which, to this day, has never run dry. There was an orchard, vegetable garden, tennis court, and more. And the lease was £65 per annum for a period of 14 years with rates of just £11 a year.

We accepted; at which point the landlord promised to have the whole house redecorated without extra charge. This was done so well that we never had to do anything more to the inside of it for the fourteen years we lived there.

It was now 1914 and in May that year we moved into our new home. We brought our housemaid, who had been with us for several years, and a nursemaid for our young children. The existing gardener and his assistant transferred to us. For the record, in those days agricultural wages were about twelve shillings a week (60p).

Our new life was almost like being in the land of Canaan, the Biblical land which flowed with milk and honey. New-laid eggs cost one shilling a dozen (5p), and the milk was the richest we had ever seen or tasted. We bought several hives of bees but, unfortunately, they all died of a disease (Acarine disease).

I soon felt the benefit of my new peaceful and beautiful environment and was a lot easier in my mind. Whether I was cheerful and truly happy I do not remember.

An almost immediate challenge was the lawns, which were extensive. I purchased a large pony-drawn lawnmower. The pony we acquired knew what to do but his hooves sank into the turf, making large holes, so we had to procure some boots for him. This led to a great game of putting them on him and it was touch and go whether the pony or we would win! In the end we did, but it was a close finish, and I could say that we won by a hoof. After this first battle, we had no further trouble and we gained the impression that the pony rather liked his boots.

And then I bought a lawn tennis outfit, net, poles, rackets, and everything one would need to play the game. Not to do things by halves, we also bought a croquet outfit. This led us to getting to know many people in the area as a result of the tennis and croquet parties and also the children's parties we often held.

We were becoming settled and content with our new country lifestyle.

But this was all about to change for the worse; war was coming.

I remember that it was while we were playing a game of tennis that the local Postmaster delivered a telegram to one of our guests. He was a Territorial and the telegram instructed him to report for duty as soon as possible. So now we knew that war was imminent. Our friend and his wife left us and went back to London.

During the following night, at 3 am, the Postmaster came again bringing a telegram telling of the dread news that Britain had declared war on Germany and calling Board Meetings of our two companies at once. Thus, our worst fears were realised.

The newspapers had been carrying stories about war for some time, so we were alerted to the general turn of events, but now it was real. To say we were disquieted would be putting it mildly; we were stunned. I bought all the leading newspapers, and they all said the same thing; if war broke out, then Britain could not stand outside the conflict and must fulfil her treaty obligations.

I remember sitting on the tennis lawn with the newspapers spread around me and feeling a sense of gloom as I brooded over the matter. I wondered if this spelt the end of my plans; what was going to happen to the business? I was worried, also, by the knowledge that we had committed to a grand and expensive scheme to open new premises in one of the best West End streets at a huge rent. What would happen now? Would all trade cease and would the business go bankrupt? What about the staff? Would they go to war? What about us? Were we going to fight for the last ditch?

And thoughts went rushing through my mind. I thought of the parable of the rich man who said he would pull down his barns and build them again but larger and with splendour, and yet his plans came to nothing.

I felt that my plans had come to nought also.

However, events marched on and eventually we decided that the only way was to go forward, hoping for the best, and dealing with each challenge as it arose. We formed yet another company, built and equipped a large new factory, and all without external capital, the whole thing being funded internally. This was a huge task, and we became short of money, but we won through.

Thus, I found myself Chairman of three private limited companies. But all that I seemed to do was attend monthly Board Meetings, inspect new factories, workshops etc. I thought that I could readily do this whilst still living in the country and by being available on the telephone as required. I would always be there to give advice.

I was uneasy about this arrangement with a war going on and felt that either I should go back to work, or else take an active role in the war. However, the consensus amongst the Board was that it would be best to remain as we were.

However, changes were happening with bewildering speed, especially when one of our two young directors, which made three in total, including a not-so-young me, said he could endure his inaction no longer and joined up as a rifleman. This was a blow to the business, but still, I did not go back.

To complicate life further, at this juncture my wife and I decided to send our eldest son to a boarding school, Taunton, later to be followed by our youngest.

Ashamed of my inaction, I joined the Volunteer Training Corps at Portsmouth and was trained to be an instructor. I did not know it then, but I do now, that my path in life was meant to be one of peace and not conquest, and that any indulgence in war-like activities would bring me much suffering.

The war dragged on its weary way, and the manpower situation in the Army became so acute that our only remaining young director was likely to be called up, in which event I would be compelled to return to take up the burden of being Managing Director of the three companies. I felt I could not do this and would rather be shot than live such a life. But if *I* joined up, it would then be impossible for the authorities to call up our one remaining director.

There was another aspect behind this decision. I felt that my life had become too easy and safe as I had previously been used to living a somewhat dangerous life in my many enterprises. I had been like a gambler and had been relying too much on just a single throw of the dice.

But now I was living a safe life without danger, and this did not suit my restless temperament.

The very idea of going back into the business actively was of concern. The thought of the daily drudgery, the same old worry cycle, from one year's end to another, filled me with loathing. I knew it would not be good for the business if our one remaining Director were to leave. Of great importance, however, was that by now I was out of touch with the day-to-day operation of the business. I only knew it as it was when I left in 1913 whereas he knew it in every detail as it was in 1916.

Thus, it was decided that he should stay, and I should join up.

To one whose life pattern was as a peacemaker, it seems now to have been a strange and foolish step to take. At the time I did not know that every entanglement in war on my part could only bring suffering.

But I know it now.

(Author's note: The business later became part of the opticians Dollond & Aitchison Ltd, which in turn was merged with Boots Opticians in 2009 having been founded by HT Hamblin (1873-1958) and traded as Theodore Hamblin. He developed his expertise as an optician and businessman during his 20s and 30s. Later, in his 40s, he became well known as a mystic and proponent of the 'New Thought' movement. See the following chapters).

Man can never experience any difficulty in directing attention to his Spiritual Source, for he is attracted by Divine Love and is ruled and governed in Love.

The Way of the Practical Mystic
HT Hamblin

Part 3

Chapter 15

I Give up my Liberty

One of my reasons for joining up was a rather quixotic one in that I thought that, as I had lived rather a bad life, I might make amends by dying for my country. I had no desire to kill Germans. Instead, I was quite determined not to kill any, even if I was given the unlikely opportunity, although I thought it would be a rather fine idea if they were to kill me. This idea seemed sound prior to joining up, but once in the Army my attitude changed, and I became as determined as others to put on my gas respirator in time and save my skin.

It took me some months to get into the Army as at first, they said they did not want anyone over the age of 40; it was then 1916 and I was aged forty-three. They would not even accept me for a role in mechanical transport (MT).

Anyway, my gardener, who was much younger than me, also felt that he should join up as both his brother and stepfather had done, but I thought this was not such a good idea as I considered that his mother should be left with at least one son; her other son and the stepfather were in the infantry and, from all I had heard, their chances of surviving the war were small. So, I thought it best if my gardener signed up for a safer role in the MT business. Because he did not know how to drive, I taught him the basics by giving him driving lessons using our car. When I considered he was competent, we decided that we would go together to join up. *(Author's note: there were no driving tests in those days.)*

We joined a group at the recruitment barracks and undertook various tests as drivers but we all, except one, failed, and this included one candidate who had already secured a Royal Automobile Club certificate and was therefore probably of a higher standard than the Army staff conducting the tests. The only person in our group who was accepted had taken the precaution of taking the sergeant, who was doing the testing, to a local hostelry the evening before.

We returned home licking our wounds and wondering if we should try again.

I then thought that my gardener would be best served if he were able to join a new branch of the Army and I coached him further with a view to him being accepted into the Royal Flying Corps (RFC). One of the skills he would need for this was to be able to ride a motorcycle. So one day I went to a colleague who possessed one, with a view to borrowing it. It was of a rare vintage and riding it was like trying to control a bucking bronco; it made me think that it was a more dangerous activity than flying aeroplanes. However, after some practice on it my gardener friend passed and was accepted into the RFC.

This left me waiting and then I heard that men over the age of forty were now being accepted as drivers of mechanical transport. I applied and was accepted; it was clearly quite a different story now as the Army needed all the men they could get. Things were indeed grim across the English Channel.

I had to pass a medical before I could be accepted and when I was examined by the Medical Officer (MO), he had a quick glance at me and my papers and said: "What on earth do you want to join up for, at your age?" He tried to talk me out of my plan to enrol but found me determined and unwilling to change my mind. At this he said he could only award me a low-category medical, but this did not suit me at all as I had no intention of messing about on home military service. I responded that nothing less than an A1 category would suit me; I wanted to help by driving lorries up and down the front lines and at least do what I could to assist the war effort.

At this he burst out laughing, in a good-natured way, and said, "Well, have your own way." then marked my papers A1, and wished me good luck.

As usual, I had got my own way, but I wondered as I left whether I was going down the right path.

I was then in limbo but in due course a date for me to report for duty came. In the few days I had spare, I spent time at home with my wife and children and did my utmost to do as much of the gardening as I could. But already I had started to reflect on my decision to join up as an Army driver and it occurred to me that a local French taxi driver with local knowledge could do more than I was ever likely to achieve.

Still, what I had done could not now be undone. The only thing to do, therefore, was see the thing through and, in doing so, I adopted an air of nonchalance and outward happiness, which did not in any way reflect my true emotions.

My wife met this unexpected change in her life with the same steadfastness she had exhibited with all the other varied changes with which I had filled our married life. I expect she wondered why a man of my age and infirmity, who was still to recover completely from a near breakdown, should want to enlist in the Army. However, she said nothing about it and went on calmly preparing to look after everything in my absence.

Soon the inevitable parting came, and, after many farewells, I went off to the appointed barracks. A last wave as I rounded the bend in the road, and I had started on yet another experience in life. I was to be a Private in the Army.

I cannot recall what the true motive was in my mind in making this huge change; maybe it was a love of adventure and change, or maybe my cowardice, which made me run away from the responsibility for three private limited companies. On the other hand, it might have been my dislike of working in London, coupled with a love of being outside and able to move freely without great restriction. If it was the last then I certainly got all the fresh air I wanted, as the driving seats of Army lorries were unprotected from the elements. I had plenty of movement too as I was to be constantly carrying things hither and thither.

On arriving at the barracks near Lewisham we were taken to the Grove Park depot where we were issued with uniform, underclothing, boots, and more. Whether the clothing fitted seemed to be of no concern to the people who issued it.

Next, we had to pass a further driving test and mine was done using a large Daimler lorry. Although it was very different to driving a small car, I passed my test and was given a temporary driving licence.

Next it was inoculation and vaccination against various ailments, but I do not recall what they were. And then, finally, we were issued with further kit including a sheepskin coat, which we all disliked as it was heavy and uncomfortable.

At last, the moment came to begin our journey to the war in France. It was a tortuous one even by the standards of those days. First, we were taken to Kempton Park Racecourse, where a few of the most experienced drivers were put in charge of driving a brand-new Peerless lorry fitted out as a char-a-banc to take us all to the docks at Avonmouth. We did not find ourselves on a ship but instead were put to work in the docks as labourers, before being taken to Southampton on a cold winter's afternoon a couple of days later. There we were put on a troopship destined for Le Havre. It was an eventful voyage: gale-force winds nearly shipwrecked us, and technical problems with the ship's engines necessitated all Army personnel being transferred to a minesweeper to complete the voyage. It was probably quite exciting, or would have been had I not been so seasick. I thought, *If this is what the Army is like, what a good thing it was that I did not join the Navy!*

And that is how we reached Le Havre.

But there is still more to the story. It was midwinter 1917, and we were allocated tents at the top of a hill with the temperature below freezing. It was so cold that when we washed our mess tins, they became covered with ice before we could dry them. One young man I remember decided to wash his hair, but it froze solid before he could dry it. As for food, we had no cooks and no cookhouse. Some of our party did their best to make a bully beef stew, but I will prudently not recall what it tasted like.

We were not the enemy as far as I knew, but we were kept behind barbed wire, although after 6pm we were allowed out for a period. I paired up with a piano tuner who happened to be in our group, and we found a delightful small café where an obliging old lady kindly fed us. I felt a little bit guilty, as I thought of the other fellows still in the camp who had to subsist on frozen bully beef and hard biscuit, every bit as hard as dog biscuit. They were all much younger than us, though, and would have coped and certainly not starved.

This went on for a week with us having to sleep in our clothes because of the very severe frost and the fact that we were each allowed just 2 blankets each. And then, with no notice, we were ordered to fall-in and were kept out in the freezing cold from 5 pm until 10 pm when we were marched to the railway station. We were then on a train, without heating, for about twelve hours; that is how long it took for it to reach our destination of Rouen, a journey of less than 60 miles.

Having arrived, it was a long march from the railway station up a steep hill to the depot we were destined for. Having had practically no food for two days and no sleep on the train, I was near total exhaustion, especially being over 20 years older than most of the other men in our group. Several times I lay down on the snow and fell asleep immediately, only to be roused by others around me who pulled me up and put me back on my feet to continue the march.

On arrival, it was not until we had completed extensive

administrative procedures that we were finally allowed to have a meal. But it was well worth waiting for and, as instructed, we took a plate in each hand, and one was filled with stew and haricot beans and the other with a generous helping of prunes or figs with milk pudding. We were all famished and for once the meal was excellent; we were all exhausted and conversation was minimal. I felt so refreshed by the meal that I was ready for a walk in the town. In fact, I felt in better form both physically and mentally than I had been for ages.

It was in Rouen that we found that the driving tests we had passed at Grove Park were not recognised by the Army in France and that we would all have to do the tests again as well as a written examination. We duly took our driving tests, and one of the aspects the Army focused on was double de-clutching. Some of us knew the trick, but many of the most experienced drivers did not and therefore they failed the test and had to go to St. Omer to be taught how the drive a lorry the Army way!

The written part of the test involved us sitting in a hut with various questions being written on the blackboard which then had to be answered on the sheets of paper we were given. Strangely, most of the experienced drivers were failed because they had no experience of having to answer such questions and did not seem to understand what was required of them. They too were sent to St. Omer to be taught how to drive a lorry and probably how to answer test questions.

The peak of this farce was reached when it was announced that the piano tuner and I, who had had no experience of lorry driving, were classed as first-class drivers while the experienced men were failed. That was how they did things in the Army in those days.

The first thing I realised after I had joined up was that I had given away my freedom. I, who for nearly 20 years had been my own master, being the head of my self-created businesses and obeyed by everyone, now found myself being ordered about, shouted at, and cursed at by any young upstart who had been made a temporary, acting, Lance-Corporal. This was a rather severe discipline, but I did my best to fit into the framework of my new life. Although I enjoyed change, I had certainly got a major change this time.

Getting used to Army food took time and, in many cases good food was ruined by its cooking; there were occasions when the food was excellent, but one could never predict what was to be served and how edible it was. Overall, it was awful.

Another thing which tried me more than anything else were the Army-issued boots. To me, the weight of them seemed to be colossal and they were stiff and markedly irritating. I was unable to move easily when wearing them and felt like a decrepit labourer worn out by a lifetime of exertion. Those awful boots had a depressing psychological effect on me as they made me feel clumsy, helpless, and very old. I felt like a convict shackled to a heavy weight. I am sure that I would have felt a hundred percent better, livelier, and fitter had I been allowed to wear a pair of correctly fitted light boots.

During my time in France, my health played up again and I spent several weeks in a hospital followed by a Convalescent Camp. It is an interesting story and has a connection to my later life as a mystic.

I was stationed at an advanced base close to the front line and was getting a bit fed up with having to do frequent guard duty and being up all night and then having to work the next day as usual, without any rest or sleep. I felt that this could not continue and, as I marched up and down my appointed beat, with a rifle over my shoulder, I thought I should ask God for sleep and rest. It was a foolish thing to do as prayer can be very powerful. My demand was based on self and not on service to others and was unwise. What I demanded from God the Infinite was a warm bed and sleep instead of so much guard duty at night. I got both, but not in the way I had anticipated.

In a few days I found myself in hospital with the word 'pleurisy' written on my card. Also, I found that a notification of my hospitalisation had been sent to my wife, by telegram, telling her that I had been hospitalised and that, if I died, she would be promptly informed. This worried me. I therefore insisted on writing a letter to her at once. The hospital Sister said I must not attempt to do any such thing as I was much too ill, and that she would not post it anyway. I objected and insisted on writing the letter, in which I said I had a mere cold, and, moreover, persuaded her to post it for me, saying that, if she did not, I would get out of bed and do it myself.

I heard Sister telling the Medical Officer that she had to humour me because I was fretting so much, and I then realised that I had overstepped the mark. I was most annoyed with myself for bringing the trouble of my hospitalisation on to my wife. She had quite enough to endure without this added anxiety.

Clearly, at the time, I was aware of the power of the mind, but did not know how to use it correctly. I had a lot to learn.

Other anecdotes from my time in France are few but there was much speculation by other drivers as to who I was and what I was. The Cockneys refused to believe that I was a Londoner because I spoke only standard English and not Cockney, but they were kind to me and accepted me as a good fellow despite my queer speech. This may have been because I had learnt to speak without affection. There were one or two drivers who spoke with what was termed an Oxford accent. They said "Thanks *awfully*" or "*bettah*" rather than better. But we all got along well.

Once I overheard them talking about me and they concluded that I was a curate; the biggest joke of all was that they thought I might be a singer! I think not…

Towards the end of my time in France, I became very thin and weak. From 12 stone on my arrival, I was now nearer 9 stone and was permanently tired, and this led to another strange experience. I was travelling with a mate in a lorry, he was driving, and I was the rear lookout sitting in the back of the vehicle. Well, I was supposed to be sitting, but I was so tired that I lay on the floor and fell asleep, after which I had a very strange experience. I seemed to go up and up, leaving my body behind, but after some time felt as though I was floating downwards like a falling leaf back and into my body. When I woke up, we were back in the lorry park, and I was back in my body after this deep sleep only to find that it was my driver mate prodding me with a stick who had roused me.

After that, I had many other such turns, until at last it got so bad that at times I had great difficulty in keeping in my body at all.

And then, quite suddenly, my life changed completely, and it happened like this.

It was a Sunday in February 1918 and we had been out in the lorry all day and returned at about 9.30 p.m., very tired and very hungry and glad we were finished. As soon as we had parked up, however, an orderly came up to me and told me to report to the Orderly Room at once. My mate and I wondered what might be wrong, for never had we known a lowly Private to be summoned to the Orderly Room at that time of night. So, wondering what the issue might be, I went as requested to be met by the Sergeant Major with some papers in his hand. He greeted me in an unusually friendly manner and said: "Hello Hamblin, have a look at these papers".

I opened them to find that I had, in effect, been requisitioned by the Air Ministry and that I was to be discharged from the Army and transferred to the Royal Flying Corps and given a commission. I understood that I was to be involved in a technical branch related to the work that my companies in London had developed.

Then the Quartermaster came in and added his congratulations and, in turn, the Officer in charge of our section congratulated me.

The next morning, very early, I was on the leave train to Calais and, after a bit of waiting around, we sailed, and I was stepping ashore at Folkestone barely two days after being told of my change of fortune. Thence I had to travel via London to report for duty at Farnborough, then to be told that I was to have eight days' leave. Therefore, I returned home to Bosham.

After the "out of body" experience in the lorry I do not recall having any further such events. Perhaps it was just tiredness, but I think there may have been more to it than that.

Naturally, I was delighted to be home again and especially pleased to have been given a commission, having never even thought of applying for one. But I wondered what the powers to be would do with me if I found myself unsuited to the new post. I knew that my health had deteriorated appreciably in the years since I first started in business with nothing and had enjoyed the excitement of living on the edge of bankruptcy until finally achieving lasting success. When I was engaged in these enterprises I was at my happiest and felt better in every way. It was when it was all over, and a measure of safety and prosperity had been achieved, that I began to lose interest.

My time in France revealed that I was not suited to driving the heavy lorries the army used and, as time passed during my time involved in the war, I noticed that I was suffering from headaches, general lassitude, and fatigue, which made it difficult for me to think clearly. The result was that I again felt unsure of myself and increasingly underconfident. However, my new appointment and commission represented a challenge and with it a share of problems to be resolved; I knew from experience that I thrived in such situations. Smooth sailing did not suit me, but storm and struggle did. I was eager to start my new role as an officer in the Royal Flying Corps.

My short leave over, I reported back to Farnborough only to find that the unit I was posted to had gone on exercise somewhere and were living under canvas. Unfortunately, no one at Farnborough knew where they had decamped to. I searched likely places in the general geographic area, and followed up suggestions I had been given, until eventually I found it. Everything was in a state of chaos. Fifteen hundred men had gone missing from the section I was supposed to be in charge off, and, to cap it all, my papers had been lost. I had no idea what my role was supposed to be, and nobody else had any idea either.

My prospective overall commander at the Air Ministry was Colonel Moore-Brabazon and I was told that only he could give me my instructions. Alas, he was ill and I was told that I must wait. So, I waited. After a few more days of muddle and excitement, I was given instructions and, having found the men who I understood were in my section, then moved the whole unit to Blandford to live under canvas.

By now it was after the first of April 1918, and I found that the Royal Flying Corps had now become the Royal Air Force.

There followed more waiting, but still nothing happened; this did not suit my disposition at all. I knew John Burrough's poem *Waiting* off by heart, but I was in no state of mind to adopt its suggestions literally. Therefore, I decided to try to find out myself what was happening.

I thought I would begin with the Squadron Headquarters and went in to see what I could find out. The chaos and muddle were indescribable; no one seemed to know anything about anything, and no obvious attempt was being made to deal with the situation. As far as I could ascertain, urgent letters and telegrams were being ignored and just put in piles and there was no logic as to what went in each pile and neither did anyone seem to care.

Fortunately, one of the clerks took an interest in my search and promised to look for the document that related to me as, without it, I had no idea what role I was supposed to be filling. I saw him the next day and he'd found nothing but, good news, on the third day he met me with a triumphal smile and produced a small pile of telegrams from the Air Ministry enquiring about me and asking if they knew where I was, and so on. These documents relating to me were at the bottom of a very large pile of unanswered telegrams and letters.

At which point the clerk now addressed me as "Sir" and, having had no training on how to be an officer, I told him he need not bother with the "Sir" bit. He replied that he had to, because I was already an officer in the Royal Air Force, although I was still dressed as a private in the Army. The conversation continued and I said that while I might be an officer on paper, I certainly did not look like one. I looked more like a scarecrow, dirty uniform, and those dreadful boots!

Soon I was armed with the necessary documents and was being recalled to Farnborough and, on my way to the railway station, found I had time for a meal and had my first decent one in a week. The Royal Air Force catering was deplorable and compared most unfavourably with the indifferent standard of the Army.

At Farnborough I was seen by the Commanding Officer who said, with a sigh of relief, "I'm glad you have arrived at last, Air Ministry have been telephoning me several times a day to ask if you have turned up and, if not, why not. I'm glad it is all over."

Then it was obvious he was looking at my worn out and crumpled Army uniform when he added, "You must be a man of some importance, otherwise the Air Ministry would not be so interested in you or so worried about your non-appearance". I assured him that I was as much puzzled by the Air Ministry's action as he was. He wished me good luck, gave me a railway warrant, and a week's leave to visit my tailor and have my uniform made.

I have no idea what happened to those dreadful Army boots.

There is nothing in the world that can make me afraid. I am established in God, upheld by the arms of Divine Love, and have behind me the Supreme Power of the Universe.

The Way of the Practical Mystic
HT Hamblin

Chapter 16

Reaping

I was able to visit the official tailors in London, who measured me for my new uniform. This was in early April 1918 and the fusion of the Royal Flying Corps (RFC) and the Royal Naval Air Service (RNAS) was not yet complete, although the official date of the merger had been 1st April. However, I was instructed by the Air Ministry to obtain a new Royal Air Force (RAF) uniform. There seemed to be a similar level of confusion reigning at the tailors as that I had encountered at Blandford. They certainly had no knowledge of the official Royal Air Force cap badge or where to obtain one; it appeared that there was only one in existence and that was the sample submitted to the Air Ministry by Gieves'. In the end my tailor used this sample.

With the rest of my leave ahead of me, I went home again to my wife. Little did I know it then, but a dark cloud lay ahead in our lives, and we would soon have to endure a journey together down a dark valley of grief.

Time passed quickly and it was at the end of my leave, just before I was due to return to London to collect my new uniform, that our telephone rang, and it was the village Postmaster to say that he had an urgent telegram for me and suggested that he read it over the phone to me to save time. Naturally I concurred.

It was bad news; our second son was ill at school in Taunton and the message was from the headmaster, who advised that our son was seriously ill and that a specialist had recommended he undergo an operation, and would we give our consent to it. We telegrammed our consent, for there did not seem that there was anything else we could do. Then my wife packed her bag and took the first available train, whilst I had to go to London and thence to Farnborough. It was a dreadful and challenging time for both of us.

My new uniform was made in khaki in a shade similar to that used by the Army and the Royal Flying Corps. No one at the Air Ministry had yet thought of using a blue-coloured cloth. My uniform was, therefore, a prototype, but it looked impressive and created a sensation, for I received more salutes than anyone else. I loathed it and the attention it engendered, and that was even before I had reached Waterloo station to travel to Farnborough.

When I arrived at the Guardroom at Farnborough the duty guard at the gate was rather taken aback by the middle-aged person just arriving who was wearing a uniform that was quite unlike anything he recognised. He referred the matter to the duty officer, who in turn informed the Commanding Officer and, in no time at all, I was welcomed by the Commanding Officer, who said: "You're Hamblin, aren't you?" I said that to the best of my knowledge I was.

Then he laughed and told me what the duty officer had told him and added: "It's your strange new uniform that did it". He asked: "Is this what we will all have to wear?" and I replied that I assumed that this might be the case. At which he responded: "Come in and show your brother officers" and led me into the Officers' Mess, which was the very first time for me. This I found to be a rather challenging situation, having had no previous experience of such an organisation and no training in its customs and traditions.

The Commanding Officer introduced me to the assembled officers and asked them what they thought of the new uniform that, in due course, they would all have to wear. They did not like it and said so. Their typical remark was: "Will we really have to wear such a thing?" I responded that assuredly they would unless they could persuade the Air Ministry to change its mind. At this point their interest died down, but it was only shortly after I first displayed the new uniform that the fledgling Royal Air Force adopted a light blue for its uniform instead of khaki.

That night I slept fitfully and could not stop thinking of our young son and how my wife was getting on, and what the future held.

The next morning, I had to report formally to the Commanding Officer. As I approached the Orderly Room the Sergeant Major was parading his delinquents and when he saw me coming, he called his squad to attention and gave me an impressive salute. It was that uniform again.

When I looked at the day's orders, I was concerned to find that I was scheduled to give a lecture. I had no time to prepare for it, and soon found myself in the lecture hall with a substantial audience, which included the Commanding Officer and the Chief Instructor. What a position to be put in; giving a lecture about a subject about which my knowledge was purely what I had learnt whilst developing businesses dealing with optics and vision. I relied in the businesses for technical expertise from those I employed who had such expertise. The Royal Air Force clearly assumed that I was an expert!

Fortunately, the audience knew less than I did, and my lecture went well.

The Chief Instructor closed the session by saying: "Very good, very good indeed". This was encouraging, but I had my doubts as I could see that I would probably be asked to give more lectures and was acutely aware that I could say little more than I had given in my first one. I had talked myself out.

But this was not to be as, at about lunchtime, I was handed a telegram telling me that my son's condition was now critical and asking me if I could go to be by his bedside. I went immediately to the Officer Commanding, and he was most sympathetic and said, "Go immediately". He provided a car to take me to the railway station. I was at Taunton the same day.

There I found my wife very troubled, for our boy was no better despite having had an operation. The surgeon told me that he had been unable to reach the seat of the trouble, in fact he had not even found any clues.

The next morning the headmaster sent for me and was in great distress. He said, "Your boy is no better, and something must be done. Couldn't you get a second opinion? So I sent a telegram to a clinic in London asking for the best diagnostics man to be sent at once; he came very swiftly. He made his diagnosis and said that another operation was essential. The specialist surgeon who did the first one came again and operated but still the cause could not be found.

Thus, there was nothing more my wife and I could do but wait for the end.

As was my habit, I started making demands on God the Infinite, in the same way I had done before, which had always been successful, although so doing had not always turned out to be the best thing in the long term. However, after a time I abandoned my pleas to God as I had a feeling that so doing was not the right thing to do in this case. Deep down, I knew I was up against something too big to be dealt with in this way and knew then that I must allow the situation to work itself out and take its own course.

Our beloved son, Dick, passed over at 3 o'clock on the morning of the sixteenth anniversary of our wedding day.

We were allowed to bring his body home. It was then that we both received an assurance that all was well. I am sure it was God speaking to us.

When he was alive and well our son Dick, "little Dick", as my wife often called him in later years, was like many other boys of his age. When he was in his coffin his face displayed a luminous beauty that was not of this earth. Our Vicar at Bosham, who was a great friend of us both, especially at this time, said that he had never seen anything like it. It was as though our son's angelic counterpart had come to comfort and reassure us that all was well.

It was a cold winter's day when the funeral took place, which was sufficient to give me bronchitis yet again. I made only a slow recovery and, when still not fully fit, received a message from the Air Ministry asking me to return to my work at once, but this time to fill a different appointment. They added that if I could not report for duty immediately then I should do so as quickly as possible. My doctor was most unhappy about this but, under pressure from me, acquiesced.

So I went, feeling more dead than alive, and took up my duties. At first the work was interesting and challenging as there were issues to be overcome as well as the construction of a new technical building which was my responsibility to supervise. It was a well-planned project but, for a reason I never discovered, no one had specified that an electrical supply should be installed. We finished up doing it ourselves! Once everything was completed, as usual, I began to lose interest in it and felt I needed a new challenge, but my appointment required me to ensure that the whole operation ran smoothly on a day-to-day basis.

Then the Armistice was declared and all I then wanted was to be discharged and go home, but this was not immediately possible. However, as was usual with me each autumn, I succumbed to a chest problem and was sent home on sick leave. As soon as I saw my own doctor, who had himself just returned from service with the Royal Navy, he was most concerned and said that on no account was I to go back to Farnborough as I needed an extended course of treatment. This course had no curative effect that I could ascertain but just made me feel dreadful, so I told my doctor that I would cure myself.

He was intrigued and, of course wanted to observe my progress.

Within a month I was much improved and could easily run a mile, whereas previously I had been so exhausted that I could walk only a few steps. Somewhat facetiously, I told the doctor that I was making rapid progress under the care of "Dr Hamblin".

In due course, I was discharged from the Royal Air Force.

Many years later, after The Science of Thought work had become established, I happened to meet the doctor again and he himself now needed help. He had heard of my work and said: "I have heard of some wonderful tales about you; you are going to put doctors like me out of business". He added that, since people generally refused to change their thoughts, they would continue to need conventional doctors. But, as the good doctor was a committed non-believer in God, my approach would be of little or no help to him. Sadly, he died relatively young despite extensive treatment for his condition by a psychotherapist in London.

Throughout this time my thoughts naturally dwelt on our own great loss and, even when it was clear that nothing could be done to save our son and that he would die, his death still came as a great shock. Regardless of what we did, including having the greatest doctors and specialists to attend to him, nothing could stay the inevitable. I felt I was up against an inexorable power or fate which all the skill and knowledge of experts could not overcome. It was a shock to my self-assurance. I had fallen on my feet so many times that I had become overconfident and believed that, regardless of any difficulty, I would always come out on top.

For the first time, I had to admit defeat. For most of my life I had looked on myself as always being the victor and was ill-prepared for this disaster.

As I reflected on events, I could see that my joining the Army was a mistake. I realised that my role in life was to be that of a peacemaker and not as part of a war-making organisation. In my case becoming mixed up in war was akin to opening a door through which disaster could enter an otherwise well-protected life. I thought about the story of Job in the Bible which tells of a man, Job, who is described as a good man who loved God. Satan challenges God, saying that Job is only good because he has a happy life and is protected. God allows Satan to put Job's faith to the test by causing him to suffer. Job never learns why he suffered, but God restores his health and gives him twice as much property as before, more children and a very long and prosperous life. I wondered if I had just been through a similar experience. Hitherto, I had been protected and always fell on my feet, no matter what foolish things I did. I could see that, by getting mixed up in war, even as a non-combatant, I opened a gap in my protection thus allowing disaster in.

Although this is how I rationalised the tragedy we had been through, I could not reason why my wife should suffer this great loss and sorrow, which is always hardest for a mother to endure, when I was the one who had erred in his ways. All my life, especially in my earlier years, I have been irresponsible and unreliable and thought that my own mother's oft repeated remark "Unstable as water, thou shalt not excel" had a ring of truth about it. It was not so much that I did not excel, as I had achieved conspicuous success on several occasions, but it was my character that was unstable. I lacked a clear purpose in life. On reflection, life had been too generous to me as I had succeeded where better men had failed.

It took a big blow and much suffering to reorientate me.

It was because of this blow that I began to think seriously about the deeper things of life, and this led directly to my later work in creating *The Science of Thought* and all its many aspects. Whereas I spent only a few years involved with each of my earlier enterprises, the rest of my life was and remains devoted to the spiritual realm. My earlier enterprises saw me staying just long enough to become established and pay their way, after which I would become bored and move on to another adventure. By contrast, my work with The Science of Thought will continue throughout my life". *(Author's note: and for very many years after he died.)*

But at this stage of my life, having just finished my time in the

Royal Air Force, I had no clear vision of what I was going to do. When I had left my business a few years earlier, I thought that I might live a quiet life in the country. The War stopped all that, but now I was able to engage in country pursuits and live a life of leisure.

But I was not cut out for such things. I had no interest in hunting, shooting or fishing, and had no desire to play golf. I did a little cycling and sailing and played some tennis, but soon lost interest in all such things. The reason was that I was at my happiest when doing something constructive and solving the associated problems but when it was all over, I became disinterested.

It seemed odd to me that all my life I had longed for and dreamed of living in the country, amid beautiful surroundings, to be able to grow fruit and flowers, sleep outdoors in the summer, hear the birds sing, be near the sea, bathe in it and sail on it. And yet now that I had all these things, and more, I was bored. Instead of being filled with satisfaction, I was restless. It was a great puzzle to me.

I was discovering what countless others had found before me, that it is in the struggle in which satisfaction is found and not in the prize when it is won. If we strive for worldly honours then, once we have them, they may still appear to be enticing or full of promise but are nothing but illusion and disappointment. When I realised this, I sought, instead, the simple joys of life and then I found that even these failed to satisfy my restless spirit.

Later I realised that someone with a pioneering spirit, like myself, can never be satisfied unless they are pioneering, creating something new. Someone who invents a new machine is unlikely to content himself with just maintaining it for the rest of his days; he will go on to invent yet more machines. That is in his nature. It is the role of a different type of person to carry out the maintenance function.

I had once been told by an adviser who specialised in identifying character traits that I was not the type of person to settle down or play for safety but must always be ready to strike out to create something new. He said that if I settled down and did not pursue new ventures when the occasion required, I would suffer. He added that if I launched out when life so demanded, I would never be a loser and would always come out on top.

However, we are not all pioneers. For every such person, there must be many others who will be content to just keep things going.

That is the way of the world.

Life must be a continual winning through, both in things practical and outward, and in things spiritual and inward.

The Open Door, HT Hamblin

Chapter 17

The Start of the Science of Thought

A year or so after I left the Royal Air Force and returned to being chairman of the three companies I had founded, it was clear to me that my heart was no longer in the business, and I did not feel that I should stay mixed up with it in any way. I knew deep down that I wanted to live an entirely different life although I had no idea what form it would take. It was now the year 1919.

Thus, I was paid out and left the companies, and at once I felt free with life and the world before me. I had given up a secure income, abandoned a safe life, and now faced an uncertain future. In some ways I felt like an explorer seeking new lands.

Immediately I did this, the sense of futility I had felt from being safely provided for, with nothing to do but live a life of existence, left me. The old pioneering spirit returned once more and with it, the zest I thought I had lost forever.

What I had done looked very foolish from the worldly point of view and those who knew me were aghast at my stupendous folly. To give up a substantial and secure income in exchange for a modest capital sum, which might only last for a year or two, was the most foolish thing they had ever heard of. They thought I had gone mad and, when my name was mentioned, some tapped their heads in disbelief to indicate what they thought of me.

There was no doubt about it, I was foolish in the extreme, and quite mad by any normal standard, and at times I woke up in the night and thought of all I had thrown away which was now benefitting others who were "reaping where I had sown". The old question popped up: "What of the future?" The future was, of course, in God's hands and He was leading me in a strange way, at least strange to me, and it felt like my life had become an open book in the mind of God.

Many friends wondered what I would do next as, without an income, it would clearly be impractical to remain in the same large house at Bosham with its 3 acres of garden and two gardeners. Logic suggested a move back into a town where I could find employment and earn an income, which could be impossible to secure in the country. How was it all going to work out?

I stayed put.

And I started to write.

My first creation was a booklet I wrote, *The Message of a Flower,* and this is how it came about.

One spring morning, after my retirement, my wife picked some daffodils and hyacinths from the garden and, having arranged them in a vase, placed them on my writing desk so that I could admire them. They fascinated me and carried me into a new world of beauty, order, and perfection, to which they belonged but to which I was then a stranger.

This triggered me to write about them and soon I had written what became the first chapter of the book. When I had completed the first short chapter, I read it over to my wife who gave her approval. Encouraged by this reception, I offered it to a "New Thought" magazine in the USA and they published it and then came back to me for more, so I wrote another chapter, which was well received, and again they wanted more, at which point I wrote all the other chapters to complete this little book.

Having been published in the USA I was soon contacted by Americans, including several who were prominent in the "New Thought" movement. One was Henry Victor Morgan, HVM to his friends, who took the view that I was a kindred spirit. This feeling was reciprocated, and we became the greatest of friends and in our communications, he became "Dear American Henry", and I became "Dear English Henry". Thus, I became known in the USA before my writing had been published in Britain.

I bought a typewriter and tried hard to master it, but my only success was wearing out several ribbons. I never became proficient and, despite my extensive practising, I was never able to type as easily as I could write by hand. Also, I discovered that I could not think clearly when using a typewriter.

I discarded the machine and instead engaged a professional typist and dictated letters. When writing a book or articles for *The Science of Thought Review*, I found it best to write in pencil and then have it typed into a neat manuscript.

In no time at all this new enterprise had grown and it needed more working space. The solution was to buy two new Army huts from the Army Disposal Board, and in April 1920 we achieved this and they were erected in the garden. Now I could begin to write seriously.

I sat down and wrote although I had no clear idea about what I was going to write about. My mind was full of possibilities, but I still had no clear concept of the direction my new work would take me.

Overhanging my thoughts was the loss of our son and the check this placed on me in what had been a wild career. By now, I realised that good can come to us only when we follow God's Divine pattern for our life. If we follow any other path, even if we are successful in business or a profession, and if we fail to follow the Divine pattern, we can face eventual ruin and disaster.

Life had dealt me some severe blows which jolted me to think rationally and face up to reality. What was the object of my life? Was it to get on and make money? In my case the answer was clearly "no" to both, as I had found from experience that this did not fulfil me or bring happiness. Was it to live happily in the country? Or was it just living for my own satisfaction? Again, it was a "no" to both as they had also proved to be unsatisfactory.

I wondered what the real meaning of life was. I had tried many things, but none led to satisfaction. Of course, we cannot see the pattern of our life in advance, and this only becomes clear as we progress through it step by step. We must learn from experience and live by faith and, until the way ahead becomes clear, we must grope our way through it. I learnt, eventually, that the solution was to trust God, stay by his side, so to speak, and progress into the unknown having complete faith in Him, God the Almighty.

When I decided to start writing seriously, in my little wooden hut in the garden, I had by then read several books about "New Thought" and kindred subjects, but never found ones that were as clear and helpful as I wanted. Neither had I come across anyone who was anywhere near as interested in the subject as I was. There was no one out there to help me, either by way of books or with personal instruction.

I had no option but to work things out from my own experience.

In doing so, I had no desire to formulate a new philosophy but, rather, I sought some method of integrating all the many factors which make up an individual life and the forces which can act on it. I knew from my own case that my troubles stemmed principally from a lack of stability. I knew, also, that I needed to become more steadfast and focused regardless of the pressures on me and what frame of mind I might be in.

The religion I had been brought up in did not help me. Although I had found that it assisted me in good times, it provided no assistance or support when I felt down and depressed. I have concluded that this was due to the religion being based on feeling and emotion rather than reason. I now know that the feeling part of me was over-strong and not in balance with the reason part of me. I had overcome insuperable difficulties in making my way through life, which meant using my strong sense of feel, because it is this which enables us to do and dare and get things done. But my ability to reason has always been weak.

Those who taught me the sentimental form of religion with which I was brought up often seemed to be sick and unhappy themselves. But they consoled themselves and others with the assurance that everything would be all right after they were dead. This seemed to be the central idea, to be nicely dead, and this was the essential tenet, after which everything would be lovely. No matter how weak a character one might be as soon as death came along everything would be perfect.

I wondered about this.

In my younger years, I remember at church we would sometimes have a great preacher who would deliver an inspiring sermon where the packed congregation would hang breathless on his every word. It was all emotion and sentiment. Naturally, we would all feel very good at the time but, after we went home, we would most probably revert to our normal behaviour and the effect of the sermon would fade in a day or two. In my experience, this did not lead to stability of mind as our feelings and emotions do not need arousal, but rather should be guided, checked, and controlled.

True religion should stabilise the character and personality, thus helping to prevent the individual reacting unduly to emotions. Emotional nervous energy should not be repressed but instead, it should either be gratified or directed into useful work; no benefit comes from ignoring it. For example, when we become very angry, we can either react physically or we can direct the same energy into some form of useful work.

This is not intended to be an attack on sentimental religion. Far from it, and I would encourage all those who are helped by it to continue and develop their lives around it. My trouble was that such practice did not assist me.

I had absolutely no intention of formulating some new religion, but my idea was to encourage a clearer understanding of the teachings of Jesus. I remember telling my father that I could not accept the doctrines in which he believed and that my main reason for saying this was that Jesus never taught them. Jesus said much but, in my father's view, obeying the teachings of Jesus would be beyond us and that we should believe by faith rather than understanding, and accept an associated concept of imputed righteousness.

To my mind, the teachings of Jesus are as clear as a bell, and anyone can follow them. In contrast, the teaching my father wanted me to accept was complicated and difficult to understand; it seemed to lack justice, fairness and common sense. At least that is how I saw it.

Also, and this is the most important point in my experience, my father's religion was not practical in my view; it certainly did not work for me. What I desired was something practical; something that would work, here and now, in this life. When I once suggested this to my brother, it fuelled his ire as he considered that I was promulgating a very wicked idea. Everything, so he said, was reserved for the next life. "After we are dead", seemed to be his motto.

From this, it follows that my family regarded me as an outcast and a pariah because I had dared to debunk their religion, which for me had proved to be of no practical use. I was looked upon as being peculiar and odd, a misguided creature, and quite outside the pale. This did not worry me as, from my earliest years, everything I have done, or proposed to do, has been condemned as wrong. It seemed that nothing I embarked on was regarded favourably by my relations.

If I had paid any attention to them, I would never have done anything with my life. Thus, when it came to religion, I took their opposition to my views as a matter of course and was, in contrast, encouraged by them.

I mention all this to show how my mind was working at the time and to help explain why I came to break away from the tradition in which I had been brought up. To me that tradition was erroneous as regards the Truth as taught by Jesus.

There is another factor I must mention and that is, as I write this in 1947, that some of these ideas are still being promulgated by a few senior churchmen. For example, the other day I read a sermon, which was reprinted in a high-class newspaper, in which the preacher claimed that Jesus was no good as a teacher and should not be regarded as such. The preacher emphasised the fact that the Apostles never once quoted the sermon on the mount. This statement was made despite the Bible being clear that Jesus' ministry was a teaching and healing ministry. The Apostle Simon Peter gave his testimony in John 6. 68 when he said: *"Lord, to whom shall we go? You have the words of eternal life"*.

Sad to say it, but my deduction is that the preacher in question, and possibly many others, was fearful that we, the common people, might go direct to Jesus to find the words of eternal life rather than going to them, the ordained ministers, for help, which could comprise a complicated interpretation of the simple message of Truth as proclaimed by Jesus. The Truth is quite clear from His teachings and in most cases does not require interpretation.

For centuries, the core message of Jesus has, in some cases, been obscured by established religion so that the teachings have become wrapped up in dogma and creed. For centuries the common man may not have had access to the teachings of Jesus, partly due to the inability of many people to read as well as the then available translations of the Bible being written in old English. For example, an older version of the Bible states that Jesus, in Mark 1:15, said *"The time is fulfilled, and the kingdom of God is at hand: repent ye, and believe the gospel."* But current translations have changed this to: *"The kingdom of God has come near. Repent and believe the good news!"*. To my mind this message is quite clear and does not require interpretation. The word "repent" to me means changing your mind and not just apologising.

The word "repent" in Greek is "metanoó" or "metanoia", which means to adjust *your* perspective or to *change your mind*. You may be going one way but pivot your thinking and bring it into line with the teachings of Jesus.

What I needed was something practical to underpin my thinking and my writing. It was changing one's thinking which became the core of my teaching, as I knew from my own experience that it really was the key. If we change our thoughts, we give a new direction to the subconscious mind which is the key to successful achievement. It is by changing our thoughts that we can give stability to our character and thus enable us to control our feelings better which can then result in us feeling more purposeful.

With that as the background, it is time to look at my experience as a writer.

When I started to write I was not at all clear what I wanted to put down on paper and had no clear plan for the structure of my proposed work; in other words, I was disorganised. I got around my problem by writing down my thoughts and, when I had reached about 20 pages, clipped them together in a bulldog clip and hung them up all round my office. I carried on writing and, when I thought I had written enough, had them typed out, and then put the pages in the correct order and sent them off to the printer! The resulting book, *Within You is the Power*, became very popular.

In writing I found that I was full of ideas, mostly chaotic, but putting them down on paper helped me to clarify them and then assemble them into a logical order.

I was not a natural writer and had to work at it.

When I wrote *Within You is the Power* my thoughts were along these lines: I had been brought up to adopt the idea that all power was vested in somebody else, or in our circumstances and environment, and never in ourselves. If I had followed that idea, I would never have climbed out of the poverty into which I was born. What I had discovered for myself was that there is a power within us which is greater than the circumstances we find ourselves in, which we can harness to rise to better things. I had learnt that this Power lies within each of us and we merely need to harness it. If we think that the power resides in circumstances rather than ourselves, then we will remain a slave to the circumstances we were born into.

This book shows the path my life took to rise from poverty to a position in which I could have had anything that money could buy, until the time I stepped away from my businesses. I had learnt that I had the power within me to achieve my goals; this was the key.

I have read many books on how to become successful which were written far better than I could ever hope to do. But, on closer examination, it was clear that the authors were unsuccessful themselves and, to my mind, they lacked credibility when they claimed they could help others to become successful. One such person used to get his message across by going on speaking tours and then telling people how to be successful and prosperous, but I learnt that he had to borrow money so that he could travel to the next town! Another man I knew of had failed at everything and had the idea of writing a book about success which, of course, was the one thing he knew nothing about.

This encouraged me to think about how I could help people by arousing in them a realisation that the power they needed for success was latent within them. I would be saying that this power did not reside in another person, their teacher for example, but in them and that they should not be put off by their own circumstances.

I had never come across a book teaching how to achieve ambition and be successful in life, and I thought it was high time a book was written by a person who had struggled in life and succeeded. My idea was to do so and show how it can be done by the spiritual power which lies within each person, rather than by using just their innate ability.

In my writing, I did not restrict myself to writing about rising above any limiting circumstances a person might find themselves in but broadened it to explain how the same power could be applied in other ways, for example, to address character weaknesses. As already mentioned, I had found, what I call sentimental religion, not at all helpful in this respect. Also, I already had much "feeling" in my make-up and the sentiment and emotion I had derived from conventional religion had proved to be of no help to me but rather made things worse. Consequently, the metaphysical approach suited me better. Statements of Truth enabled me to reach and maintain rational control over my undisciplined "feeling", which is, in reality, the subconscious mind.

But what did I mean by Truth, spelt with a capital T?

To find the answer to this question entailed much thinking. If I could not find an explanation, then all such things as statements of Truth and affirmations were merely self-deception. I had no one to help me and had to reason it out for myself.

After much study and contemplation, I realised that this conundrum had been solved by the Ancients. In Ecclesiastes 1:9 is the statement *"The thing that hath been, it is that which shall be; and that which is done is that which shall be done: and there is no new thing under the sun."* Indeed, there is nothing new. That is a great Truth.

Looking back, I am not sure how I arrived at this deduction. I had certainly never read anything about Truth in books and there was no one I could discuss it with, so perhaps it came to me in a dream. I shall never know.

Of course, those of you who have read my writings will have absorbed my message about Truth but when I arrived at the understanding, it came as a great liberating enlightenment. It made everything clear and logical and would be readily accepted by the subconscious. If we make statements of what we hope to be true, the subconscious will reject them, for it will only accept that which is true, and which we know to be true.

The explanation is this: there is a real world of perfection of which the present world is but an imperfect reflection and is also disordered and imperfect. There is, however, perfection in Eternity. When we make a statement of Truth, we are referring to the world of perfection and of the person who lives his true life close to God.

Jesus said: *"If you can believe, all things are possible to them that believe"*. (Mark 9:23). In colloquial language one might say: "It is time to open your mind."

One can almost hear Jesus saying this and, in our own imagination he might have added words to say, in modern language, that within each person rests perfection which merely has to be activated. Change your minds and your thoughts.

Do not think in terms of the part of the world you occupy and of its disease, sickness, sin, and its limitations, but instead focus your thoughts on the way the world was intended to be by the Creator, with everlasting perfection and purity.

I once read this:

Nothing is too good to be true
Nothing is too good to last
Nothing is too good to happen.
(source unknown)

And quoting from Robert Browning, we could add: *And the best is yet to be*. In other words: "Only good can come to me".

And I had embarked on my mission to explain the Truth aiming to do so in as simple terms as possible.

Our work is not the healing or curing of diseases of the body, but rather their prevention through the finding of God's inward peace and joy of His salvation.

We cannot even begin to find God's inward peace, until we have forgiven to the uttermost.

His Wisdom Guiding

HT Hamblin

Chapter 18

The Science of Thought – Huge Challenges

Having published my first, and very small, book, *The Message of a Flower*, I wrote and produced my next and called it *The Power of Thought*. Of the thirty or so further books I wrote, the one which met with the greatest demand was *Within You is the Power*. This demand was probably a function of its title for that alone epitomised the New Age movement.

The old idea was that all power was vested in someone else, in other words in an exterior person or organisation, and in the current world this has given way to the new idea that the real power lies within a person and that all things are possible. (Of course, this was not a new concept to the saints and mystics of the past.)

Also, the old idea of a wrathful God dispensing punishment has passed. Instead of a God of wrath, envy, jealousy, and revenge, we now believe in God being love, order, wholeness, harmony, and absolute goodness. We know that we are not punished by an angry God because we have sinned, but that instead, because we have fallen short of the Divine order of God, we have punished ourselves by falling into disorder. We know that God does not condemn us, but instead we know that we condemn ourselves when we depart from God's intended order to find our own satisfaction and gratification from sensation and desire.

The more we seek satisfaction from sensation, the more we will suffer. But this is not due to God's anger and punishment, but because we try to satisfy our soul's longings for worldly things rather than turning to God who is the fountain of all good things.

Jesus said that His Spirit would be *in us* like a well of living water carrying us into everlasting life. The Spirit would not be outside us, not in somebody else, but *in us*.

God does not condemn us, and we should not condemn ourselves. Self-condemnation is as harmful as condemnation of other people. Remember what Jesus said, when a woman was taken in adultery: "He that is without sin among you, let him first cast a stone at her" (John 8:7). Thus, Jesus was challenging his onlookers and there was not one of them who was guiltless. They had wanted to stone the woman because they saw in her a reflection of their own sin, but they slunk away one by one.

Then Jesus turned to the woman and did not condemn or lecture her or tell her that she was sinful. Instead, he said to her: *"Neither do I condemn thee: go thy way... sin no more"* (John 8:11). The moral of this story is that we should never indulge in self-condemnation because God does not condemn us but merely says *"sin no more"*.

The New Age teaching is that God is Love and can only be Love and only does things that are Love in action. (Note: The word Love, with an initial capital, is often used by some to signify Godly Love rather than human.) The New Age teaching is nothing new and is simply a return to the teaching of Jesus who, in the Lord's Prayer commands that if we forgive others who have sinned against us, then God would also forgive us our sins against Him, God. *(Luke 11.14 "And forgive us our sins; for we also forgive everyone indebted to us. And lead us not into temptation but deliver us from evil.)* This means that God's mercy and forgiveness is always active, and could not be otherwise, because God is the very epitome of Love. In other words, whilst we retain an attitude of unforgiveness, we cannot align with God's mercy and forgiveness, but that, as soon as we forgive other people, then we will be in the right frame of mind to feel the embrace of God's mercy and forgiveness.

This does not mean, however, that because God's power lies latent within all of us, we are self-sufficient. The Power is indeed within us. The Kingdom of God is within us. But this Power is not of our making but is the Power of God. Of ourselves, we can do nothing, and without God we are nothing. We *are* because God *is*.

We are totally dependent upon God. Of ourselves, we cannot love God or even be interested in Divine things. It is the Spirit of God within us which recognises and loves God, for only God can truly know God.

Also, it is my belief and conviction, that, although we may think that we are planning our own life, experience shows me that God has designed a pattern for our life which emerges as our life unfolds. This Divine pattern is perfect and therefore, if only we would or could keep to it, our life too would be perfect. One of the expressions I used when *The Science of Thought* commenced was *"our life is perfect as imagined in the Divine Mind"*. This was and remains a very powerful statement. There is a perfect world of reality, this being the expression of the Divine Idea, which has created a perfect path of life for us.

Understandably, it is human nature not to follow this path initially and instead we want to take our own self-created route. Therein lies the cause of many of our troubles and sufferings.

Now to my writing. Quite early on I realised that most people would not benefit from their copious reading of books. As an example, one man wrote to me to say that he had some fifty New Thought books, but he did not seem to feel any better for having read them and felt that he had made no progress. On further communication with him, it was clear that each book taught something different, resulting in the poor man's mind being a mass of undigested and conflicting ideas. What was needed, I thought, was a course of lessons which would simplify this new teaching, prune it severely, and also strip it of its occult practices.

Then, I thought, by presenting just one facet of Truth at a time, and by restricting the student to that one idea as well as encouraging him to put some of the advice into practice, he or she would make progress. It is my experience that, it is only when we put into practice the Truth which we already know, that we can make progress. If we practise what we already know by using our conscious mind, and find it works, then that will confirm that the statement of Truth we are using is, indeed, true. This stepping-stone approach really works.

If we use what I call "head knowledge", it is unlikely to be successful as it remains only intellectual theory. But when we put knowledge into practice and find it works it gives confidence, and we learn in a powerful way. We then know the Truth.

With this thinking behind me, I produced my first Course. It was not very spiritual as it dealt largely with advising the pupil how he or she could extricate themselves from what I call the rut of circumstance. However, although it lacked a strong spiritual dimension, it did put some people on the right track. Some even went so far as to say that the advice in the Course brought about their conversion, in the spiritual sense, and awakened their souls. This may have been strengthened by one slogan I advanced which was on the lines of "The old life is dead; enter a new life of victory and power". My memory is not precise on this, and it may have been more like: "I have entered a new life of overcoming and victory".

When I wrote my first Course in the early summer of 1920, I had to work out how to sell it. With care I selected several magazines and periodicals and advertised in them all principally to offer our books with the Course as an additional option. For the record, the magazines were *The Strand, The Windsor, Pearson's,* and others, and I recall the rate was £70 per issue. Hugely expensive by the prices of the day.

As I had only started work on this new project in April of that year, I clearly wasted no time and worked like the proverbial galley slave, early and late, and cannot now comprehend how I managed it all, but I did!

The announcements in the magazines duly appeared, but orders for the books we were already offering flowed in only slowly. With each book sent out we included a prospectus about the Course, but time passed and there was no response. But then an enrolment came in from someone in Oxford. This was in August 1920. It seemed to me that this solitary enrolment marked a turning of the tide. Until this point, money had been flowing out like the tide, but this solitary enrolment showed that it was now going to flow back in and, once again, the scepticism of my relatives and friends would prove to be erroneous.

They had good reason to be sceptical of my new venture and suggested that it was doomed from its very beginning. Other people, they reminded me, had tried to run similar businesses from premises in towns with all requisite facilities around them, but had achieved scant success. By contrast, there I was, tucked away in the heart of the country and without experience either as a teacher or as a writer, with no knowledge of writing, or publishing, or of postal correspondence work. And, to cap it all, they reminded me that what I was attempting to do was entirely new and that I had no one to promote me to a public which knew nothing about me.

By conventional standards the whole enterprise was doomed to failure and was such a strange venture that it could not succeed. I too had my doubts as I realised the enormous task ahead of me. It seemed to me that starting a business in the West End of London, with almost no capital and yet making a success of it, was mere child's play compared to what I was now seeking to accomplish. I realised there was an enormous challenge ahead.

But still I went on; it was a venture of faith.

Consequently, when this solitary enrolment from Oxford arrived, it affected me profoundly. I was not filled with the type of shallow optimism one feels on achieving even a modest success which can evaporate when a small reverse is encountered. Indeed, I even joked about it, saying that at any rate we would now at least be able to say that we had received one enrolment. Our effort had not been entirely without purpose.

But when sitting quietly by myself, I again experienced that same feeling of peace and elation which I had experienced previously in my life and which in each case had been a harbinger of success or good fortune.

Emboldened by this I went forward as Joshua had done when the Bible says in Joshua 1:8: *This Book of the Law shall not depart from your mouth, but you shall meditate in it day and night, that you may observe to do according to all that is written in it. For then you will make your way prosperous, and then you will have good success.*

Whenever my mind was invaded by thoughts of discouragement, pessimism, or failure, I would counteract them by cultivating thoughts of hope, optimism, and success. I found it particularly helpful to think about the way God had delivered me previously from difficulties, especially when such deliverance seemed to be near impossible. I found that if I reflected on God's deliverance, and in the way His love had manifested itself in me in the past, and if I assured myself that what God had done previously, he could still do the same now. A feeling of liberation would then engulf me, and the burden would be lifted, and I would experience something akin to what St Paul meant by these words: *"that the creation itself will be liberated from its bondage to decay and brought into the freedom and glory of the children of God"*. (Romans 8:21)

I felt assured that things would get better and that I would be able to proceed with this new venture and felt refreshed and encouraged.

I am quite sure that no one ever started out to try and teach Truth who was so ill-equipped as I was when I commenced this new work. I had heard it said that one of the best ways to learn is to begin to teach. In my case, this was certainly correct because I found that trying to help people overcome their problems engenders a clarification of one's own thoughts and ideas, as well as deepening one's understanding of Truth.

The first enrolment was quickly followed by others and, in no time at all, additions had to be made to the office staff and buildings.

It was soon apparent that this first course was too advanced for many people who had subscribed and, therefore, I brought out others which were simpler and focused on the power of suggestion to help overcome many of the difficulties of life. This kept me very busy and, as the enterprise developed, I found that I was working as hard as or harder than I had ever done before.

It soon became clear that there was going to be a significant demand for the type of advice I could supply. It was clear too, that what so many people sought was Truth presented in everyday language in a simple and clear form.

However, I was troubled that my course of lessons was not of a sufficiently spiritual character. They certainly helped people make a success of their lives and overcome problems sufficiently to become happy and contented. But I was becoming bothered that I was neglecting the importance of the spiritual dimension.

A friend of mine advised that I should keep going the way I had started, as most people are not cut out to be saints or be godlike. He added that the average reader has no desire to become a saint and has no desire to become one, and it would be counterproductive to advise them otherwise. This was the clear advice my friends and supporters were giving me and no doubt what they were saying was quite true, but I still had a nagging urge to scrap all my Courses and write them again but with a more spiritual focus.

As usual I did not do things by halves. The sensible thing to have done would have been to keep on with the existing Course while preparing new ones to replace them. But I was not built that way and was always single-minded and determined. For me it was all or nothing with no half measures.

I withdrew all the Courses in stock and refunded the payments but, despite this, more and more people asked for them. Another madman's action you may say, and I was often referred to a being "As mad as a March hare". But then I was born in March so there may be some truth in this!

On reflection, though, it was indeed a mad action, because the Courses were our principal source of income and the receipts from the sale of books did not even cover the cost of promoting them. Thus, it was clear that my action in withdrawing the Courses was the height of folly as it left me with continuing large outgoings and no income to compensate and, on top of this, I would incur the additional expense of preparing new Courses.

Having made the decision to withdraw the old Courses I did not do it by halves; I made a thorough job of it. I took them to the top of the garden, arranged them in a hollow square, and then set fire to them. They burned for days, and I stood for a while after lighting the fire and contemplated watching hundreds of pounds going up in smoke.

Folly of the first order, you may say. Yes, from a human standpoint I agree, but the Spirit was urging me to do it as a preliminary to writing the new Course. In my life, following the Spirit has never led to disaster. Each time I have taken such a radical step, which looked disastrous at the time and threatened disaster and ruin, it has led to amazing success. I hoped the Spirit would be right again this time.

I did not know then that the new Course was going to be much longer than the first one (twenty-seven lessons) or that it would take me so long to prepare. I worked on it early and late every day and, naturally, it took longer to duplicate having so many lessons in each Course. Also, I had to write a book to promote and explain the Course and this proved to be quite hefty; this cost a significant amount of money to get printed and, as it was to be given away free, it was a substantial overhead to cover.

The writing of the new Course was a challenge, but I was fortunate in having amazing inspiration; once I had started work on it, I could not stop the project as it had a life of its own which buoyed me along with it.

The problem, though, was in the promotional book. I worked early and late when writing it, and again seemed to be under a spell of inspiration but I was not sure if it was true spiritual inspiration. Having written it I sent it to the printers, passed the proofs, and when the print-run had already begun at the printers, I instructed them to stop work on it immediately. More madness on my part and delaying the book could jeopardise the entire project but, without the promotional book announcing it, no one would be aware of the new Course. Surely, it was the very zenith of folly?

But I knew that the Spirit must be satisfied and had been uneasy about the book even when I was writing it. I was still uneasy when I corrected the proofs. But after I had passed them for printing, I began to have one of the most uncomfortable times of my life. I wondered what the cause of this could be. I thought that it might have been the promotional book, but I had put so much work into it, and really thought it would be a real winner, and did not want to face the challenge of rewriting it.

However, at last I did face up to it and, as soon as I did so, I knew it was the book which was the cause of all the trouble. The Spirit wanted me to alter it, and I knew that to refuse the promptings of the Spirit would lead to difficulties. I had no wish to grieve the Spirit, which would in itself be a great disaster.

As soon as I had stopped the printing and decided to rewrite the book, God's peace came to me, and I felt liberated and relieved.

Naturally, the printers were upset about it; a literary colleague who had helped me write it was also upset but, on my part, I reverted to my usual optimistic and confident manner.

I got the book back and rewrote it. I toned it down, and one of my critics who read it thought that this had spoilt it, but that did not trouble me at all for the only thing that really mattered was to be in harmony with the Spirit.

After this delay the revised book was printed and circulated and achieved excellent results.

Every time I have followed the prompting of the Spirit the result has always been all that one could hope for but whenever I ignored these promptings, the result has been unsatisfactory.

The saga taught me that I was liable to come under the wrong kind of inspiration, which was not the Holy Spirit, but of some darker influence. This darker, Luciferian influence no doubt coloured quite a lot of my earliest work. This is the reason I was so anxious to destroy the old Courses, when conventional prudence would have advised otherwise. My soul was restless until I had destroyed them.

That drastic way of dealing with such a situation suited me; I find that I always work better when I have burnt my boats behind me.

This chapter, however, only deals with part of the story. There was another big move on the way, which, combined with the saga of the Course destruction and the new promotional book, strained my financial resources almost to breaking point. Indeed, at times, it was only the most rigid self-control and the strictest right thinking which prevented me from panicking.

Something more than steadfastness and resolution was required in such a situation and what it needs is trust in the ever-present guiding Spirit. The Spirit knows the Divine pattern of our life and is always seeking to guide us into alignment with it.

Only with the Spirit's guidance can success and satisfaction be found.

It was time to move ahead again.

The reason man is so weak and helpless,
and his life so barren
of beauty and true achievement,
is because he works entirely in the Seen,
and ignores the greater life of the Unseen.
Man is constantly striving in the world of effect and neglects the greater world of cause.

The Message of a Flower

HT Hamblin

Chapter 19

The Science of Thought Review

On top of what could be seen as my incredible folly (by conventional human standards) in destroying all copies of my first Course, came the crowning act of starting a monthly magazine. Clearly, I was not satisfied with all this destruction, not the least being upsetting my printer by halting the production of my book, but there was a clear signal that a magazine was needed.

It was not my idea. The idea for the magazine came from several of my students who said that they would welcome one as it would be an adjunct to the main work of teaching through the Courses with their many lessons. Also, they said, it would enable the work I had commenced to become more widely known.

I knew nothing about producing a magazine and was not worried about the prospect. In all my various occupations previously, I had taught myself and felt that I could take on tasks about which I knew next to nothing. It meant that I had to learn the processes of editing, managing, selling, and distribution and do so in a short timescale.

The more I thought about it, the more I liked the idea. The first steps were to select a suitable name for this new production and determine its size, format, price, and style. Once these issues were settled, I then had to do all the writing. And then the next task was to arrange for its distribution both through trade outlets and direct to customers. This was a huge addition to my workload and I was yet to find out that it would entail me having to answer letters from readers in addition to my considerable existing tasks.

I thrived on it.

At last, all was arranged, leaving only me with the task of doing all the writing. I had no clear idea of what to write but I wrote, and wrote, and wrote, and still the magazine was not full. Therefore, as I had not yet established any potential contributors, and lacked office staff to undertake the related work, I filled up the blank pages with extracts from other magazines of the "New Thought" type, with due acknowledgements.

Before launching the magazine, I sent a letter to all our students, asking if they would like a magazine started for their benefit, and if any would like to become subscribers. About twelve hundred replied that they would. This was very encouraging as I knew that various previous attempts by others at running a magazine of this type in the UK had only reached this figure after several issues. If we could start with such a number, I was sure that we could quickly increase the circulation, if only by word of mouth.

With confidence, I had no less than ten thousand printed, which pleased the printer I had previously upset. Of this total, some twelve hundred went to those who had subscribed, and the rest I gave away, just keeping a handful back for stock. Who they went to I cannot recall but I know that subscribers distributed copies amongst their friends, and this resulted in more subscribers, and in no time at all we had a substantial number of people requesting their own copy.

I well remember the day I took the payments from the first subscribers to pay into the bank. In those days, payment was normally by postal order (PO) and when I took some twelve hundred POs of seven shillings and sixpence to the bank *(38p),* the cashier looked at my suitcase full of them, and then at the paying-in book, and then at me, with a look of pained surprise and, uttered under his breath: "The Post Office people *will* be pleased to see this lot".

It was soon clear that what I had started was an international business and this gave us the difficulty of dealing with many currencies. Our auditors explained the problems this created for them, and the solution was simple: I set up our own currency exchange. Thus, we opened a Foreign Currency Account at our bank and, when foreign currency was paid in, our Currency Exchange converted it to sterling. In this way the organisation dealt only in sterling. This arrangement continued and has worked smoothly ever since.

The Science of Thought Review began its full operation in October 1921 and has continued without a break ever since. When we started, many long-established clients for my Courses sent words of encouragement and congratulation and wished me God speed. They also told me that they would pray that I might be given strength for the task ahead as they could foresee great responsibilities and temptations. I wondered if they likened me to a rocket and feared I might come down like one?

I was not too concerned, as I have had responsibilities before but have never found it to be a burden. I have also endured temptations but have regarded them as no more than initiations which, if successfully passed, have never held me back. If we pass them successfully then we proceed; if we fail, then we must accept it. My attitude has always been that, if we succeed, we give the credit to God and, if the reverse is the case, then we do not complain, because it is our fault for not following God.

As *The Science of Thought Review* progressed, a band of writers gradually gathered around me. One was a retired seafarer, and there was another who wrote for children and then another who wrote on healing topics and who was really a metaphysical practitioner. There was one very special acquaintance I made, however, and he was Richard Whitwell, a writer of mystical books and of like mind to me. Strangely, he was introduced to me by a person from the USA who was visiting the country. I shall never forget when they visited me together, as they had decided to do so by walking some 15 miles over the South Downs *at night*. This reassured me, as I then knew that I was not the only rather mad individual around!

The result of this introduction was that *The Science of Thought Review* became a publisher of Richard Whitwell's books and he himself became a regular contributor to the magazine. We became firm friends.

Soon after the first issue of the magazine was distributed our subscribers started to send us more money than we needed and, for example, where we would have expected less than a certain amount, they rounded it up. We, therefore, started a special fund to deal with this extra money and called it The Free Literature Fund. Since that was started, we must have sent out millions of leaflets, pamphlets, books and more, all supplied to readers and students for them to pass on to others.

As more and more money came in by way of donations, love offerings in effect, I established another fund which we called "The Magazine and General". This enabled the magazine subscriptions to be reduced by nearly 30% thus making the magazine affordable for almost everyone. We had a similar arrangement for subscribers living in other countries. But we went further; those who could not afford even the reduced price of the magazine were given it gratis with the costs borne by the Fund. And then we went further still and ceased asking a fee for the Courses and instead requested donations.

From the beginning of the Courses venture, I had been bothered about having to charge for them and it was a relief to be able to change this and rely on donations instead of demanding recompense. This tradition has continued, and to this day, the work operates at a loss which is more than balanced by donations. The result is a harmonious operation with everything coming to pass at the right time. It is a matter of faith; the right people appear when they are needed and things which are in short supply come our way.

But of course, until one learns and trusts this way of doing things, one must pass through a period of trial and error and then it is necessary to test that everything works smoothly. I would like to give you examples of the progress we made but, as I never kept a diary, this is not possible in any detail. What I recall is that the experiences I had as regards the supply side, such as money, were challenging. But once I had won through each situation, I thought no more of it. The advantage of having this ability is that one thinks no more of the stress and sleepless nights involved, the wrestling with the angel, the getting up in the middle of the night to have a walk in the garden, the anguish and despair. All this is forgotten.

I thank God that He has given me this ability to put a challenging experience behind me and effectively erase it from my consciousness. It is a huge advantage. The disadvantage is small; it just makes it difficult to remember the trial and tribulations of life.

However, I do recall clearly one of my experiences which directly related to *The Science of Thought Review*.

It happened like this. In 1926 it became clear that my work was now too extensive to remain in our present temporary offices and that a move was necessary. We had been enlarging the offices piecemeal by adding extensions to the Army hut we occupied but the result was not ideal. Also, the house and grounds were not my property, and, worryingly, I had never asked for permission to erect any of the huts I was using. Moreover, my wife and I thought that we would like to live in a smaller and more convenient house.

Next to us on the west side was a meadow of about twelve acres with a splendid view down the Bosham reach of Chichester Harbour to its front and of the South Downs to the rear. After negotiation, we were able to buy four-and-a-quarter acres of it.

The vendor queried why I wanted so much land and said to me: "What do you want with four-and-a-quarter acres of land, surely a quarter of an acre would be enough?" My reply was that I was a writer, that I was moody, and that I wanted room to breathe and a place where I could roam about without meeting anybody, and without having to go off my land onto a main road if I needed to have a long walk. He seemed satisfied with my response.

There we planned and built the offices *(Author's note: These lasted until the mid-1990s when they were replaced)*. I decided to have temporary buildings capable of lasting twenty or thirty years. My thoughts were that at the end of that time, we would be able to judge whether the work was likely to prove permanent, or otherwise. If the former proved to be the case, then we could erect a permanent building. If it turned out to be the latter, then the work could be closed and the building demolished.

In 1927 the offices were completed and occupied. In February 1928 we started on the house on the same area of land, and in August we moved into it. In addition to all this, we had to lay out the grounds, construct a long driveway up from the main road, and plant many trees, hedges, and shrubs.

Naturally, all this enterprise was expensive, and concurrently I had lost a considerable sum in trying to help a relative, so that I was left in a tight position financially. If one had looked at the finances from a conventional business perspective, it certainly looked as though I would have to borrow substantially to meet my commitments. The amount of money I had lost was due to my dabbling in outside affairs; would I ever learn?

The only thing I felt I could do was to move forward and not retrench. People of faith have a saying which says, more or less, "When in doubt, wait". This is to allow time for Divine guidance to filter through; in other words, we should be patient. Whilst this is good advice for many situations, in this case I was committed to a course of action which could not be delayed. I trusted at the time that if I continued, help would be forthcoming as required.

I knew that I had no serious financial problem because a neighbour, who knew nothing of my private affairs, said to me several times: "If you need financial help, just come to me". Interestingly, the amount he kept offering exactly met my predicted obligations. I was in a quandary; trust in God to deliver his "Divine Substance" which is always there, but I would have to show faith and trust in it. If I did not, then I would have to seek human help.

And this was not the only offer I had to lend me money as the lawyer who handled the acquisition of the land also tempted me with an offer to secure a mortgage. And so, it went on, first one thing and then another by way of offers to help which would tempt me to trust the arm of the flesh, instead of God and the "Divine Substance".

But I trusted, and everything worked out. Each time the builder came to me for payment I was able to pay him without any difficulty and throughout the process adequate funds were always there just when they were needed.

The result of all this was that the offices were paid for when they were completed. And it was the same with the house which was built immediately after the offices. We were never in debt. To this day I do not know how it was accomplished. It was one of those experiences which reminded me of the Psalmist: *"This is the LORD'S doing; it is marvellous in our eyes"*. (Psalm 118:23)

Most people who live by faith must admit that some things which happen to them are beyond human comprehension, and I put my experience in that category; I thank God for it.

I confess that I prefer to live a life of faith; it is exciting. It is akin to the disciples going fishing where they toiled all night and caught nothing only to be told by Jesus in the morning: *"Throw your net on the right side of the boat and you will find some. When they did, they were unable to haul the net in because of the large number of fish"*. (John 21:6). One who lives by faith finds life much the same, the Lord comes, and abundance comes with Him.

Life is certainly worth living when it is so exciting. If I ever contemplate the usual life of a secure salary, with a pension in later years, I am filled with dismay. The increasing tendency in society for everyone to become a cog in a machine is not one I could endure; maybe it might be better to die!

In these early days of my work, as an experiment I drew nothing from the business for personal expenses and we were living as though on invisible support. Something always turned up, a small legacy, borrowed money refunded unexpectedly, tax refunded, personal gifts, and so on. The "widow's cruse" never failed.

The lesson I draw from the financing of the construction of the offices and the house is the secret in the concept of "Divine Substance" involving a belief and trust in a power greater than our own which can perform the impossible. Just recall some of the miracles that Jesus performed which showed that there is a power out there greater than ours. If we do not believe that the impossible is, in fact, possible then it never will be possible; it is a matter of faith.

'The House We Built' (photographed in 1970)

If we accept that reality is just what we can see and experience, then that is what we will find. However, what we need to do is not so much deny the obvious but instead affirm that that God has other channels, which are beyond our present knowledge and understanding, which He can use to deliver what is needed.

The Hamblin offices (1928)

It was shortly after the offices and house were completed that I met Henry Victor Morgan and his wife, who both became supporters of *The Science of Thought Review* and he also became a contributor. One event that I need to record is when they asked me to accompany them to a conference in London at which various speakers were declaring that there was no Hell and no Heaven. I was called upon to make a statement on the subject based on my life in business and now as a spiritual teacher and I said, succinctly, that I knew there was a Hell because I had lived in it most of my life, and that there was also a Heaven, as I had also lived in that although only at intervals of very short duration.

This stifled further talk at this event about there being no Hell and no Heaven.

And now another traumatic event occurred…

But to have good motives and Heavenly desires is not sufficient. We must train our mind to work along Heavenly lines; for the mind and its thoughts, trained to obey the will, are the executive of the soul.

The Psychology of Prayer

HT Hamblin

Chapter 20

War Again

Things were going from bad to worse in Europe and a period of fraternisation with the leaders of Germany produced a sort of phoney peace. Britain was arming and building shadow factories and we had to learn and practise installing and using black-out on all buildings. In addition, there was much publicity about what to do in the event of gas attacks.

And thus, we sank down a steep slope into war once again, less than 21 years since the previous one.

War again. What would it mean this time? Would London be wiped out in a few hours? We did not know and could only wait and see.

All of us involved wondered how it would affect us and *The Science of Thought* work. What would we do in the event of invasion or under frequent bombing? Being at Bosham, we were in a highly vulnerable location, we were near the coast and within range of the guns of enemy ships as well as close to several military airfields and we were sure these would be targets. On top of all that, we were told that we were in an invasion area and must be prepared to retreat inland at a moment's notice.

As for preparation, we saw antiquated guns from the pre-First World War period being set up which would clearly be of limited use. Also, holes were dug at the sides of roads in which brave men were expected to hide in the hope of stopping a modern army just by using their rifles. Other measures taken included placing old vehicles and trailers alongside main roads in the hope that, should the enemy invade, they could be placed on to the roads to become obstacles. These seemingly futile preparations might have been appropriate in the South African war, which had ended 37 years before, but would surely be ineffective against the modern Army we were up against.

This demonstrated that we were totally unprepared for the war which lay ahead.

Then came the thought: "this will be a total war. Everyone will be conscripted for service of some kind; everything will be rationed, buildings will be commandeered, and all peace time activities will cease". Maybe the best thing we could do now would be to close until the end of the war.

Then came the thought that I might be of some use if I were to struggle on with the work as best I could, and this is what I decided to do. My thinking was that my work could help to support some people through the war, provided I lived long enough. And my watchword became "To help as many people as possible to weather the storms ahead".

As with the run-up to the previous war, there seemed to be a great calm. By this I do not mean the newspapers or public broadcasts on the radio, but inwardly where I felt peaceful. This was the calm before the storm. I have since learned to be very suspicious of such calms, as they always seem to presage an outburst of evil.

However, when the hard fighting began this false calm disappeared and, in its place came deep distress as I felt as though I was in hand-to-hand combat with the forces of evil, the Dark Forces.

Soon it became clear that the war was only one of many forms in which evil was manifesting itself. People were being tested and tried in every possible way, from within as well as from without, and all the time people were tempted more severely than ever before.

This applied particularly to teachers and leaders of movements such as ours. I felt strongly that efforts were being made to drag our work down and obliterate it. If it was not destroyed by one method, then I felt that another would be tried. If I, myself, could not be got at, then I was convinced that other methods might be used. We were an organisation promoting peace and this might not sit comfortably with the population of a country at war.

My soul was attacked again and again but each attack was thwarted although it often felt touch and go. Clouds of deep darkness and gloom often descended on me and could last for weeks but in each instance, I was brought back into the light. I was greatly helped by John Moreton, a writer on matters to do with the soul and religion, and his huge experience of dealing with cases where the soul of a man was being battled for by the Powers of Darkness, stood us in good stead. He was quite well known, and his books went far and wide; he was an advocate of peace.

We were sure of two things:

- This furious onslaught I was under showed that I was on the right track.
- That every time we gained a victory over the Dark Forces, we struck a mortal blow at the evil which was attacking mankind.

The real war I faced was an interior one and the only way to win was by using spiritual powers; the Forces of Light against the Powers of Darkness; good versus evil.

The spiritual war is still on, and the battle continues. There will be no true peace on earth until this spiritual warfare has run its course.

Meanwhile the physical war raged on. In the early years of it, even uttering the word "peace" could be considered by some as a crime. As I have just mentioned, I was in contact with John Moreton, the writer. This attracted the attention of the London police, Criminal

Investigation Department (CID), who paid him a visit at the offices of his publishing organisation. This CID man did not wish to detain him, but it turned out that his real interest was to find out about a mysterious man by the name of Hamblin. Who was he? What was he? What did he do? Where was he? And so on.

Mr Moreton later told me that he answered all the questions about what he himself was up to, but this, he told me, clearly raised suspicion in the mind of the CID inspector, because of the connection with this mysterious man Hamblin. The inspector demanded to see all the correspondence between Hamblin and Moreton and Moreton and Hamblin. This was duly produced by Mr Moreton, and the Inspector proceeded to scrutinise every letter, clearly thinking he was investigating a great conspiracy. He plodded on and found nothing suspicious until he alighted on the words "The Secret Place". At once he stopped and pointing at the words with his finger, asked Mr Moreton the meaning of this. What was this Secret Place? Who went there? Where was it? He must have thought he had found something incriminating at last. He probably thought, also, that his worst suspicions were justified and that he would soon have these two conspirators under lock and key. Little did I know it at the time how near I came to being apprehended as a conspirator against the State!

Mr Moreton would at this point have been in his element. He explained to the suspicious Inspector that the place referred to as the Secret Place of the Most High, was where we meet with God in the Quiet and Silence of our own soul. I can imagine that, as he explained this, a hush came into the room together with a sense of God's perfect peace, but as I was not there this is conjecture on my part. Anyway, the CID man was satisfied and decided that there was no need to arrest either John Moreton or me. In fact, John told me that the Inspector said that from what he could see, if only people would listen to what we had to say, and if they were to follow our example, there would be no wars.

Thus ended the great Inquisition, no doubt caused by my Peace pamphlet which dared to say that we should do as Jesus has advised, viz., *"bless those who curse you, and pray for those who spitefully use you"*. (Luke 6:28)

It was due to Mr Moreton's tactful and wise handling of a potentially difficult situation that I both remained a free man and had no trouble subsequently with the authorities. This was in sharp contrast with what happened in many other offices I knew of, where even married women up to the age of about fifty were compelled to move their occupation to do what was termed work of National importance.

The next challenge we faced was a rise in postage, which added £1,000 to our annual costs, in 1939 prices. Next came huge increases in the price of envelopes and paper which almost doubled in their price to us and, in addition, purchase tax was applied as well, which added about a further 20%. All these extra costs looked overwhelming at first but in practice we barely noticed them.

What did hit us hard was the shortage of paper and, although it never impeded our production, it was a close-run situation at times.

The Battle of Britain was an exciting and thrilling time and many great battles took place over our heads. German aircraft fell all around us and, sometimes, one of our own fighters. I remember one aircraft descending in flames and it looked as though it would crash on our offices, but it fell a distance away and buried itself in the ground.

Then came the bombing of Britain. My wife and I found this challenging because we had no fire watchers appointed for our premises since we were outside a built-up area and employed less than 50 people, these being the relevant criteria. So, my wife and I had to be our own fire watchers and air raid wardens. The routine was that, as soon as we heard the air raid warning siren, we got up and patrolled the property, just as a party of fire watchers would have done, had they been appointed. Sometimes when things became quiet my wife and I would stroll around the garden but at some other times, which we called sad nights, we would watch the ambulances with flashing lights and sirens drive past our gate.

Being up for several hours, night after night, proved very tiring for us both, especially as we were both over seventy years of age at the time, although we still had sufficient energy to complete our normal work each day. My wife always kept herself busy and did everything needed at home as well as being a very active member of the local horticultural society and the Women's Institute. As for myself, I worked early and late every day, had no hobbies other than writing, which I did and still do laboriously by hand; in addition, I corrected all printer's proofs myself and the many things which other people might have delegated to others. We were never a couple interested in holidays and had more than enough to amuse us at home.

Now let me move away from war for a moment and look at brighter things.

When one gets near the end of life, the feeling is that time is so short that we must make the best of such life that remains. My experience shows that living a busy and strenuous life is the best way to keep active and my wife is no different in this view. At this very moment of writing, she has just ridden off on her bicycle loaded with flowers to place on our dear son's grave. When I was in business, we kept two cars; now we have just two bicycles! It is all we need.

The humble bicycle is democratic and allows one to stop and meet people, if needed, whereas a car separates people from others.

When I established *The Science of Thought* the aim was to make it an accessible friend of all humanity and of all creation.

I would be in seventh heaven if all the birds and animals were to gather round me as I sat in the garden and I would tell them all what I treasured about them. I thought it was a pity they could never know the warmth of my love for them. If they had this ability, they might have returned in their hundreds. Alas, they would keep aloof as they did not understand.

And yet, in a spiritual sense, and below the surface, all creation is one of unity, fellowship and love. It was hard to visualise this when a war was going on, but glimpses of this unity came to me from time to time with animals, birds and with children too. I had been having these experiences on occasion from well before the war began and they continued after it had ended.

For example, one winter's afternoon, I was just starting a walk when a flock of seagulls flew inland over Bosham harbour from the sea, when I had another of my strange experiences. I felt as I was at one with these wild, free creatures flying towards the setting sun to roost. Suddenly, I realised that, in some strange interior way, I was one of these birds, flying their solitary way into the wintry sky; it felt as though I had always been thus and was securely supported by the air and could not fall to earth. Everything was in its correct place and there was harmony in everything, and I felt as though I was timeless. The present moment, past centuries, past aeons, they were all the same to me just for a few moments.

On several occasions I have felt as though I have had fellowship with other creatures and have been admitted to their world as though I was a friend and brother. I recall once meeting a red squirrel one evening when walking in the woods nearby. He (or was it a "she"?) was as surprised to see me as I was to see him. He clutched his arms around the branch on which he was crouched and looked at me with his big bright eyes. He seemed satisfied with his inspection because he made no attempt to retreat. He looked at me, while I looked at him, and for a brief spell it felt as though we were one. I felt in a state of perfection and comfort and one with everything in the Universe.

There were other occasions when I experienced a great sense of kinship with all creation, and one involved me coming across a splendid cock pheasant walking slowly across my path whilst I was out walking, whereupon it disappeared into a small wood. I quietly followed him to see where he had gone and was amazed to see him standing just a short distance from me. He was almost near enough to touch. A moment later a half-grown rabbit came along and crouched down close to our feet. This was surely a meeting of angels I thought and so we held a little prayer meeting together. I was quite sure that God heard all our prayers, and I was left with a feeling of joy and peace on earth and goodwill towards me and all feathery and furry creatures.

This was far from the only such experience I had where I felt an immense affinity with other living creatures.

Meanwhile the war raged on and in August 1942 we were bombed. As I mentioned earlier, our home was near several airfields, of which at least two were key ones for the defence of our islands, and bombs were often dropped indiscriminately all over the area. But on one occasion it seemed that our house and the offices were targeted. It was the night after the Canadians' ill-fated landing at Dieppe. During the day, my wife and I had stood by our gate to watch hundreds of Canadian tanks roll by. We waved at them, and I got rather carried away with militarism. This was an error on my part as by then I knew that I was destined to be a peacemaker, not to be a pacifist in a negative sense, but always on the side of love, gentleness, kindness, forgiveness and similar. I know that when I depart from the true path I fall into a state of adversity. Doing so would be my error.

Consequently, this momentary lapse by me into militarism opened a door to the forces of evil. I knew from experience that there were always warring forces against me, both by day and by night. Even in my sleep attempts were made by these forces to molest me, to destroy my soul, and thus destroy my work.

But hitherto, all such attacks had been spiritual and psychic; nothing had ever happened in a material sense. I felt as though God had placed a protective shield around us all, protecting us from all material danger. There was plenty of evidence of this, the incredible loyalty of my staff, the way we were supplied with all our needs at the right time so that my work was not restricted in any way despite the violence of the war which surrounded us. But I had inadvertently opened a door to evil...

Seventy-one bombs were dropped that night in our neighbourhood. I was busily writing as usual, but on this occasion in the house, instead of in my office. At ten minutes past eleven it happened. Things became so noisy that I got up from my table, left my writing and went and stood by the front door. My wife was standing guard at the door of the room where our little grandson was sleeping *(Author's note: the grandson is the author of this book!)* Then the bombs whistled down, but they all missed the house. The bombs that fell were in a direct line with the house, but the timing was slightly in error and the house was straddled between two of them. No one was injured but part of the office complex was destroyed by a bomb that fell very close to where I would normally have been working at my desk.

After the bombs had exploded, I went outside to investigate. Seeing a light, I went to look and found that it came from a small incendiary which was burning in a bomb crater; my neighbour and I put it out. We never found out how it ever got there and can only assume it landed there after the bomb had gone off.

The only damage to the offices was from a bomb that had exploded a few feet away, causing part of the northwest side of it to collapse. If I had been in my office at the time of the bomb explosion, I am certain that I would have been injured because the nearest bomb crater was only about 20-30 feet away.

As I thought things through later, I realised where I had gone wrong and allowed evil in. At the same time, and with grateful heart, I pondered how amazingly we had been preserved and upheld. I was reminded of the 23rd and 24th verses in Psalm No 37: *"The steps of a good man are ordered by the LORD: and he delighteth in his way. Though he fall, he shall not be utterly cast down: for the LORD upholdeth him with his hand".*

I have always found this to be true. If we lapse, we may find ourselves mixed up with some form of a disaster, but if we uphold this Truth we can be supported by God.

After the "all clear" siren had sounded, my wife and I spent time doing our best to tidy up; she swept up broken glass while I repaired doors and locks. After that, to bed, but not to sleep; at least there was no sleep for me. I spent the rest of the night thanking God and praising and blessing him for all his mercies. We were especially thankful that the bombs had fallen where they did because, if they had fallen on the adjacent village, there would have been many casualties. As for us, we had not even a scratch, and our young grandson, aged four at the time, did not even wake up, but slept the whole night through.

The next day there was a lot of tidying up to do, but the work was not hindered, and all the post went out on time.

A small incident? Yes, merely one of many incidents, but an important one, in that it showed me very clearly how easily one can wander and fall into trouble and yet, even when we fall, we are upheld by God.

The war dragged on. Bosham harbour, which our house overlooks, became choked full of landing craft, while every road was packed with guns and vehicles. At last D Day arrived and we discovered that our harbour had become empty, for a vast armada had sailed during the night.

After that came the V1s, Doodlebugs we called them, and we liked these less than ordinary bombing although they did not bother us much. We heard or saw many flying over to explode elsewhere, but none fell within a mile of our home.

Then came the V2 rockets. They did not trouble us at all, but we were gravely concerned about what they were doing to London.

After that came the defeat of Germany, and unthinking people imagined that everything would then be lovely. Then came the Atom Bomb. After that, H.G. Well's pronouncement that humanity had come to the end of itself and will be succeeded by – what?

It is time humanity looked to God to unravel the tangled skein of life, which continues to baffle utterly the wit and wisdom of man.

Will mankind ever learn?

The great secret underlying the spiritual development is giving and receiving. Not only must the student of the Divine Mysteries learn to commune daily with the Infinite, thus becoming filled with Divine Power, but he or she must express this Power in work, service and living.

HT Hamblin

Chapter 21

After the War

When the Second World War started, my one desire was that I might live long enough to help our people throughout the war, that is, students and readers of *The Science of Thought Review*. That task has been accomplished and, when the writing of this book is completed, I shall feel that my life's work is done.

I now have no remaining earthly ambition and my days of pioneering are over. All through my life I have sown so that others might reap. My sole desire now is that others may reap where I have sown as, in due course, I shall have to cease my work. Personally, I have never been one to do any reaping and I leave it to those who follow me to do that.

My experience is that pioneers seldom make good reapers and I have most definitely been a pioneer.

With my work as a pioneer inexorably nearing its end, I am encouraged to observe that some of my ideas are beginning to permeate established religions. But there remains much more to be done and this will fall to those who follow me in this work.

My key message is that the fundamental requirement is to follow the teaching of Jesus without dogma.

There are, however, several things still to be completed during the time I have left. The first thing to be done will be to turn the work of *The Science of Thought* into a properly constituted organisation so that my work is able to live on after I have died.

After that, I would hope that one day, a suitable new building will be erected to enable my work to continue in some form. *(Author's note: this was done close to the beginning of the current millennium but the facilities are now owned by another organisation although the work of HT Hamblin continues online. (www.thehamblinvision.org.uk)*

I do not want to retire, and I could not endure a life of idleness because I know that, if I am to avoid boredom, I must always be trying to achieve something. Consequently, I have no intention of ceasing my writing and hope, therefore, to write one or two more books. What I would like to do would be to go on working at full speed and then come to a sudden stop.

There are two ways of dying which appeal to me. The first is to lose one's life while trying to save the life of someone else; there surely cannot be any death more satisfactory than this, that a man gives up his life to save another person. The second is to "die in harness" by being hard at work right up to the last minute.

However, our lives are entirely in God's hands and what will be, will be. All we can do is to continue progressing through life and doing our duty, leaving the rest to God.

As I look back on my life, it seems very clear to me that God's purpose behind all my time has been good. To me the words of Psalm 23:6 encapsulate my feelings: *"Surely goodness and mercy shall follow me all the days of my life, and I shall dwell in the house of the LORD forever."* This is precisely what has happened to me – goodness and mercy all the way.

During the whole of my life, I was not conscious of doing anything good, but I can now see clearly that God has been consistently trying to reveal His goodness to me, and to make me realise that His designs for our lives are perfect.

Looking back, I feel as though I have, at times, been working against God and His intended designs and it was as though I was living a life that was completely removed from the pattern that He, God, intended me to lead. More than once the Godly presence has come to me seeking to show me a better way and to enable me to understand that God's Divine perfection always surrounds us even though we cannot realise or see it. Despite the struggles and strains of life, we are surrounded by Divine presence.

The great disasters and sorrows I have faced were necessary instances to encourage me to turn to God. But God, who is Infinite love, did not want me to suffer; the disasters were entirely due to my actions and behaviour as I followed a life that, for many years, was not in harmony with God's way.

I can see now that all the wrongs I have endured have been necessary. I see also that that the wrongs I have inflicted on others, which I deeply repent, have been transformed by the grace of God, the Divine, into remedial experiences for those affected.

Thus, the Spirit makes use of every condition and experience to help us back on to a path back to God. I am reminded of the story in the Bible of the prodigal son. (Luke 15: 11-32):

"Not long after that, the younger son got together all he had, set off for a distant country and there squandered his wealth in wild living. After he had spent everything, there was a severe famine in that whole country, and he began to be in need. So, he went and hired himself out to a citizen of that country, who sent him to his fields to feed pigs. He longed to fill his stomach with the pods that the pigs were eating, but no one gave him anything.

When he came to his senses, he said, 'How many of my father's hired servants have food to spare, and here I am starving to death! I will set out and go back to my father and say to him: Father, I have sinned against heaven and against you. I am no longer worthy to be called your son; make me like one of your hired servants.' So, he got up and went to his father.

But while he was still a long way off, his father saw him and was filled with compassion for him; he ran to his son, threw his arms around him, and kissed him".

For the son, the misery of living and eating with swine became a remedial experience which made him go back to his father. The parallels with my life are obvious.

It is possible to see God's hand in every new experience I have had and His Divine activity in everything which came to me in life. And what has been true of my life must surely be true of all lives. God has a perfect pattern for each life. It cannot be confined to just a few people but to all humanity, in the same way as an oak tree is potentially present in every acorn.

Therefore, my conviction is that the greatest and most effective prayer is the one given to us by Jesus and especially these words: *"Thy will be done..."*, which is equivalent to saying: *"Let the Divine pattern appear"*. By praying this prayer, we do not try to make God do anything but what we are doing is surrendering ourselves to the will of God.

Throughout our lives we may, unknowingly, have been wrestling with the will of God and probably getting the worst of it. Folly is no match against God's wisdom. But, as soon as we surrender ourselves to God the Divine, then Divine order will prevail.

But I can almost hear you say: "But we really must pray for something". I agree wholeheartedly and advise that the greatest thing we can pray for is what I call Divine Adjustment, and by this expression I mean bringing our lives into the pathway which God intends. There is no merit in fighting the will of God; instead, we must follow the path set out for us. I have found that the best way to pray this prayer is not to request things but instead to give thanks to God for everything. Every time a thought of fear or anxiety comes into our mind, we can help to overcome it by thanking God for these feelings, as they are helping us to respond to the need for a Divine Adjustment. When we pray for a Divine Adjustment what we are seeking is merely that Divine love and its associated wisdom (God's wisdom) enters our lives and works its perfect way.

At first we may find it difficult to pray that God's wisdom should shape our affairs because this might spell the end of some of our aspirations. We may fear that the things we aspire to are not, after all, worthwhile and may have to be discarded. Thus, we can become reluctant to offer such a prayer. But remember that anything which would not be in line with God's infinite wisdom will never be any good for us and will bring only sorrow and suffering. Let God take control.

If we pray for a Divine Adjustment following God's path of infinite wisdom and love, then we should certainly pray for this as it will help us achieve order and harmony. This alone will bring true satisfaction.

It is my experience that it is only God's divine wisdom and love which brings us everlasting satisfaction; Jesus called it "entering the joy". Specifically, Matthew 25:21 says: *"His master said to him, 'Well done, good and faithful servant. You have been faithful over a little; I will set you over much. Enter into the joy of your master."*

God is both Divine wisdom and Divine love, and it is only by surrendering our lives to him that eternal bliss can be found. If we seek things that are not in line with the Divine will and purpose, we will make it impossible for the Divine pattern to unfold in our lives. But achieving the Divine pattern is probably the greatest joy a person can experience.

This brings us to the vexed question of surrender. We generally dislike the term, but the enemy is one's "self" as we are reluctant to give up everything. To surrender is the last thing that our "self" wants to do, and this "self" is the enemy of surrender. It will fight it all the way. And yet, although we will arrive at the point where "self-hood" could be surrendered, my advice is not to force the issue until you are truly ready. To force the issue could be as harmful as trying to open a flower bud with one's fingers instead of waiting a few days for it to open naturally. There is a right time in the case of a flower bud, and a right time for an individual soul to open into God's Divine light and glory. Everything comes to pass at the right time but only if we allow it to do so.

This reverses the concept of prayer I was brought up with. I was taught that prayer was offered to appease God, to whom we must grovel. We had to beg and pray to him to give us what we thought we needed and then request other favours.

Reduced to a few words, what our praying amounted to was that we wanted God to do our will; we did not want God's will to be done, just our own. In effect our prayers could be summed up with this phrase: "Not thy will, but mine be done, O Lord"; the reverse of what Jesus had learnt to pray at Gethsemane.

When the right time comes for a person to surrender his or her "self" to God, after which the person begins to live more in the Holy Spirit than in the flesh, it will prove to be the entrance to God's eternal joy. The change will not prove easy but what is required is trust, trust in God's infinite wisdom and infinite love. The reward will move the person closer to harmony in all things and closer to perfection.

When I began my work, leading to the creation of *The Science of Thought,* my sole aim was to help other people along the pathway of life. I spoke of living by faith, and keeping my mind focused on God, and of overcoming hurdles and achieving eventual victory. This was satisfactory as far as it went, but it did not go far enough. In my own journey I had my own serious temptations, challenges and sorrow to overcome. If it was necessary for me to face these difficulties, it will probably be necessary for all. God is no respecter of individual foibles.

I learnt early in my journey that we do not merely have to follow the teaching of Jesus, but we must follow *HIM*. We must make the journey of Jesus in its entirety; we cannot just select the bits we prefer and forget the rest.

At this late stage of my own life, my desire is to help those people who are ready to do so to pass from bodily death into life, that is into new life in the eternal world of Spirit. The central issue is our relationship with Jesus and to his message.

There are two facets to approaching this fundamental issue. The first is the teaching for what could be called the pre-surrender stage, and then there is teaching for those who are ready to surrender fully to Jesus and follow His teachings in all that this will imply.

But when the time comes, and we surrender ourselves fully to Jesus, we must also be prepared to surrender our loved ones. Until we learn to surrender, our inclination will be to dominate God in our prayers. When we pray for our loved ones, we are in a way coercing them. If we pray for ourselves, by requesting God to do specific things for us, we are risking disorder in our life because, if we ask for the wrong things and they are delivered, we run the real risk of making matters worse. Asking for what you want may not be in line with the Divine plan. The same applies when praying for loved ones; the wrong type of prayer can make their condition worse.

The core of my message has always been and remains that the great secret of prayer is to surrender to God completely. Pray for God's will to be done in His way and His time. Do this instead of making specific requests. Instead of asking God to do this or that, the matter should be handed over to God completely by asking God to do His will. By praying in this manner, one can be confident that He will work His perfect will in the lives or situations we are praying about.

The central Christian prayer, the Lord's prayer, makes this quite clear...."*thy will be done; on earth as it is in heaven.*"

Praying in this manner may prove to be one of the most difficult things for anyone to do. It is difficult enough to surrender ourselves and our souls to God, but to extend this to our loved ones as well may prove even more difficult. We are so possessive in our love for our family that we can dread letting them go. But until we let them go, we hinder rather than help them.

God is at work in each of their lives just as He is in ours; He always has been. God has given us all free will and it is entirely up to us to decide whether or not to follow the path which Jesus set out. It requires us to have huge trust in Him and even greater trust to commend our close family into His care. It is an act of surrender, and this can be difficult to do.

Our instinct is to be concerned about them and suggest that they do this or that because of our love and care for them. In effect we do not want to let them go and feel that we should be involved in guiding them. But this approach can lead to our concern for them becoming a form of interference. When we pray for them and with specific requests, it can easily transpire that our praying amounts to interference which could increase their difficulties rather than help them. Our prayers for them should always be on the lines of the Lord's prayer: *"Thy will be done..."*

However, when we fully hand them over to God and relinquish any attempt to influence them, God will guide them in the way of the Spirit and help to bring their lives into harmony with Him. This is the most difficult lesson to grasp, and probably our greatest challenge, but we must trust all that Jesus has taught us and have full faith in God.

This brings me back to my early years and to the way we were then taught to pray where we were the victims of erroneous teaching. There was no focus at all on the need to ask God for His will to be done, rather than our will. In fact, we were taught that God was wrathful and that there were very many dreadful sins we had to avoid if we were ever to reach God; consequently we grew up to associate sin with God. This was in sharp contradiction to the teaching of Jesus, who taught that evil things were the work of Satan. For example, we were taught that terrible diseases were due to the will of God. Consequently, we feared God and certainly had no wish to invoke His will in our prayers. if, deep down within us, we had a belief that asking for the will of God to be done might risk one of the many terrible diseases which we were told as children were coming to infect us, then it might be prudent not to ask God to do anything. In this situation, it would be better to pray for God's Divine Adjustment to come into us so that we can correct our understanding of God and appreciate that He is love and not wrathful.

The term "Divine Adjustment" was not used when I was a child, but I use it extensively now as it means all that is lovely, beautiful and perfect. It is what we all aspire to and, therefore, praying to God and seeking your own Divine Adjustment should pose no difficulty. We could even alter the model prayer of Jesus to say: "...thy Divine Adjustment be made, on earth, as it is in Heaven".

Looking back at my life, once again, I can appreciate now that my real work has been to help people have a better understanding of God than hitherto. Perhaps I should say that God, by His Spirit, has awakened my consciousness so that my understanding of God has evolved, and this is directly reflected in my work and in that promulgated by *The Science of Thought*.

I can see it all now and appreciate how my ideas of God have gradually changed. When I was a child, I understood that God had to be entreated to do things. It was when I found that praying this way did not deliver results that I began to seek the true nature of God the Divine, which led to my own Divine Adjustment. Previously my pleading with God for things to happen often gave contrary results. It was then that my ideas gradually changed. Now I no longer wanted God to do my will, and no longer did I wish to choose my own path through life, but desired, instead, only that God should lead me on and guide my way so that I could help bring His wishes to pass.

Gradually, and step by step, I began to appreciate that God's hand was on everything, that His ways are perfect and that the

Divine order is always present and that our troubles are caused by our falling away from it.

If we can find the Divine order and become one with it, then we have a direct pathway to God. To attain this, our will and our life must be in harmony with God and with the Divine pattern of life. This will require us to turn fully to God.

There are many ways of achieving this and each person must find out what is best for them. For example, throughout my teaching I have stressed the importance of achieving one's inner silence. I have stressed, also, the need for inner prayer which should be ceaseless and should focus on giving praise and thanksgiving to God. Taken together I have found that, over the years, this brings about almost perfect healing.

Another factor is equally important, and that is the need to live a pure life. We must follow Jesus and be Christ-like in our inward life.

Those people who think they can live a life of sin, and then avoid the consequences by using metaphysical treatments, can be in for a shock. Such treatments can be harmful if the fundamental problem of their lives is not also addressed. They need to understand that life needs to be lived according to the teachings and will of Jesus Christ.

Metaphysics is philosophical: it's about explaining the fundamental nature of the world and what it means as humans to inhabit it. Spirituality, on the other hand, is experiential, and has more to do with spiritual practices and the development and discovery of the self. My approach has always been firmly on the spiritual side, which is a very simple philosophy as it merely requires life to be lived in the way Jesus taught us: be as Godlike as possible.

God deals very gently and generously with human frailty. If we fail because of our frailty, then, if we repent and confess our sin, God will forgive us. The Lord's Prayer is quite clear about this. But we must have a deep desire to be pure and to continue in that way.

Sin happens, alas, and if or when we fail, we should not dwell on our sin in regret but instead we should turn to the Lord and focus our thoughts on Him. If we keep doing this we will, in time, become more and more aligned with God.

It is one thing to relapse into sin through human frailty but quite another to do such a thing deliberately. The former is forgiven but the latter, if sustained, will inevitably bring a harvest of suffering or unhappiness.

When I use the term "pure" I also mean sincere and truthful. Acknowledging Truth is fundamental to following Jesus as this is what he practised and lived by, and we must do our best to emulate Him. One cannot claim to follow the Truth if our life is a living lie. Our lives should be so pure and true, and our motive so sincere, that we live by Truth. Jesus taught Truth.

As the hymn says:

Eternal Light! Eternal Light!
How pure the soul must be,
When placed within Thy searching sight,
It shrinks not, but with calm delight,
Can live and look on Thee.

-Thomas Binney (1798-1874)

When we have been purged of all the "self" aspects – self-seeking, self-interest, self-esteem, and all ulterior motives, only then can we stand before the Light of God.

We cannot hide anything from God. We can only enter the Kingdom of God when we yield up everything to Him and hide nothing.

This brings me to the end of this book. I hope that it has done more than just interest and possibly amuse you and that it will prove helpful to those travelling the road of life and who are seeking God and His Truth.

Without God we are nothing and can achieve nothing. It is His Spirit which accomplishes all things.

Now unto him that is able to keep you from falling, and to present you faultless before the presence of his glory with exceeding joy,

To the only wise God our Saviour, be glory and majesty, dominion, and power, both now and ever. (Jude 24-25)

Afterword

based on writings of HT Hamblin introducing his Courses c.1922

The greatest message I bring to you is this: that a person, by working daily for a short time in the inner and higher mental and spiritual realm, can subtract the evil from their life and add good in its place. That is to say, by meditating upon the Divine perfection they become changed into its likeness. This will also destroy that influence in their lives often called bad luck and ill-fortune and replace it with harmonious good.

It will banish unhappiness and fill them with a great joy which has its source within and is not dependent upon outside circumstances. They can protect themselves and others from danger, difficulty and disaster. This approach works with precision; one is not dealing with uncertain theories, but with immutable law which can never fail or alter. This is real prayer.

They do not do this by willpower but by harmonising with the Infinite. Real success in life is only to be found along this line of harmony with the Divine. Mankind is a spiritual creature, and when an individual realises their own spiritual nature and learns how to draw upon the Infinite powers within them by working in unity with their Divine Source, their lives become changed. Day by day a little evil is taken out of their lives, and day by day a little good is put in its place. Results are not seen at first, but they are cumulative, and in time are bound to manifest just assuredly as the rising and setting of the sun.

Many people say, "What is this evil influence that follows me? As soon as I get on a little in business, I suffer a severe loss. When I make plans for a happy life, disaster overtakes me and blasts all my hopes." There is no evil following them; instead, what they are suffering from is absence of "good" due to the disharmony of their thoughts and lives. When once the disharmony gives place to unity, then the transformation of their life begins."

But while any true system of thought-control is training the student in the techniques involved, it is also accomplishing other changes, which makes for success and stability in life. Will-power, concentration, determination, perseverance, creative imagination, directed thinking, natural memory, the appreciation of beauty, self-confidence, cheerfulness, and optimism, are all developed without the student being aware of it. I mention these things because they are of real value to the student, but they fade into insignificance beside the major objects which the practice of Truth achieves.

Epilogue

by Clare Cameron, Editor of *The Science of Thought,* 1961

The wish of Henry Thomas Hamblin was granted, as only a very short illness preceded his translation into Higher Service late in the afternoon of Tuesday 28th October 1958. There was a most unusual sunset that day and its clarity and radiance, which we like to think welcomed him, will never be forgotten.

Much remains unsaid in these pages, yet if all were told of the private difficulties, problems and sorrows which beset him through the years, and the steadfast serenity and faith with which he met them, having time for every wayfarer and every visitor nevertheless, more than ever we should know him as the saint he really was. And even more so for his simplicity, modesty, common sense, practical ability, and humour. These qualities have been the hallmarks of real saints, always.

Yet the world only knew him as the famous optician, Theodore Hamblin (the name he adopted for that business), founder of the well-known shop in Wigmore Street, London, W1, which functions to this day, and the many branches of the original firm throughout the country which, as told in these pages, he yielded up to others. It is significant that he went from serving actual physical eyesight to helping countless numbers develop spiritual insight.

The influence of his work goes on, indefinitely, for the simple reason that not only did he teach the truths of eternity but wrote from actual experience of what he had tested and proved. Despite the tributes and testimonies, we shall never know how many lives were changed, and continue to be changed, through his teaching and his example. For all who were privileged to know him, as well as his writings, recognised that he was in the tradition of the great mystics.

Author's note: The work of my grandfather, Henry Thomas Hamblin, continues to this day under the guidance of The Hamblin Trust: www.thehamblinvision.org.uk